EVERY THING IS A *gift*

John Joseph *&*
Richard Glaubman

EVERY THING IS A *gift*

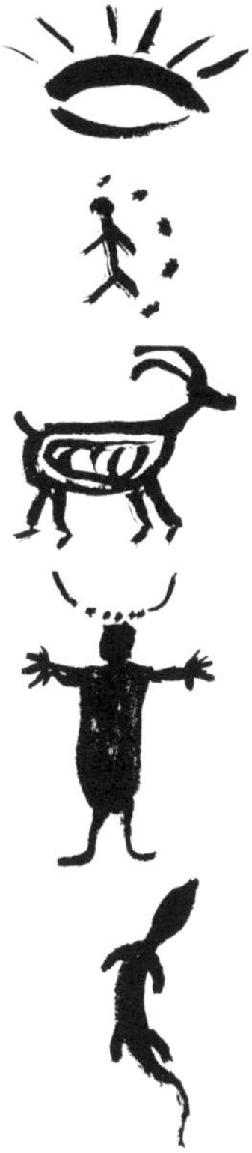

John Joseph &
Richard Glaubman

IRIE BOOKS

ISBN 978-1-51541715-6
Copyright © 2018 by
John Joseph and Richard Glaubman

Cover and interior design:
ital art by Mariah Fox

Cover photographs by Tannis Alley
and John Joseph

Petroglyph drawings by John Joseph

All rights reserved. Printed in the United States of America. No part of this book may be used or reproduced in any manner whatsoever without permission except in the case of brief quotations embodied in articles or reviews.

For information, contact www.iriebooks.com or The Editors, Irie Books, 542 Franklin Avenue, Santa Fe, New Mexico 87501.

DEDICATION

To my wife, Helen, and my grandparents, Pepé and Memé.
-- JOHN JOSEPH

To my granddaughter, Sophie.
-- RICHARD GLAUBMAN

"Everything is a gift."
-- PEPÉ

SURVIVORS

For Raymond and all veterans of war

The stench of death
Stays in your nose and mind,
Forever
When it's over, it's not over.

Flight home, cruel welcome
Home's door
No one knows,
No one understands.

So we seek each other,
Sit and stare in the pond
No words, fishing poles for props,
Sad comfort
Not spoken.

Sweat lodge steam
Burns the lungs
Steams the eyes

Already filled with tears

The scent of the Creator
Voices from stones
Tell the truth
Stone medicine
Helpers of heart
Sense of peace
Restless sleep.

The children
Grow up
Parented by
Grandma and Grandpa.

We are stamped: PTSD
We are marked: *Psychosis*
We have our Government papers
To prove it
Weird words to mark a man.

My friend Raymond 53 years old
Home from the war 30 years
Smokes two packs a day.
Whiskey his drug of choice
VA gifts him Xanax, Zoloft, Paxil

Diabetes — more drugs
Hypertension — more drugs
Heart disease — more drugs
PTSD — more drugs.

The war machine munches on
Eating what it can't digest
More drugs, more forms, more drugs
More dreams Agent Orange

More drugs, more wars,
More mirrors —

Mirrors? you ask.
Yes, mirrors, for without them
We'd be no more than
18 or 20
Hell's mirrors
Reflections of old
Early old
Decrepitude

Raymond, dead at 53
Yet he — and we —
Some of us
Survived
Agent Orange
War
Nightmare
Flashback
Job loss, person loss

Self-loss
Vision loss.

In the sweat lodge
My heart screams —
"Love you, Raymond"
Through heat haze, unblurred
Sister Virginia Miller,
Dear friend
Comes into focus.

These share and bless
Our sacrifice
In tears of heat, not hate

Out of darkness
They come, loved ones
Unblurred in sweat and tears
Blessings
No mirrors, papers,
Drugs, denials.

Mind memories
Twist and lie
Soul memories
Never die.

— John Joseph

ONE

My grandfather, Pepé, spoke a timeworn patois of French and Mohawk dialect that was once used along the Mohawk trail with French and British fur traders. The fur trade had disappeared generations earlier, but Pepé still spoke in that dialect. Pepé was a cabinetmaker, working all his life with maple, birch and oak from the hardwood forests. But when a traveler from the west placed a plank of knotty pine in his hands he discovered a new world. He rubbed his hands along the length of the plank and said, "This is a soft wood, but it is beautiful."

I was too young to use the sharp chisels and saws that hung on the walls of Pepé's shop, but I was allowed to be in the shop and play in the sawdust. I watched as my father and my uncles who were also cabinetmakers passed the board around. When the board came back to Pepé, he said, "We need to work with knotty pine."

We lived in a small house nestled against a natural rock formation. One of the boulders was even bigger than the house. My Uncle Gerard would take me up on that boulder and recount the days when wild animals roamed the Mohawk trail that went by our house. But there were no wild animals left, the forests were dwindling and Uncle Gerard said, "We must prepare for our journey."

My grandmother handed me a canvas bag that native people called a "possible bag" because we put everything in it that we possibly could. I asked, "What should I pack?"

"Choose what matters to you, but only take what you can carry."

I went out outside, unfolded the bag, turned it upside down and shook it. A piece of wilted lettuce and a dried-out green onion fell to the ground. I walked among the big rocks and picked up two stones. Pepé stepped out of the house and I asked him, "Which one should I take?"

"Take the one that speaks to you. The rocks, the earth, even the sky are all gifts from the creator." Then he handed me an empty coffee can and said, "Your father and our fathers before us walked on this ground. You can take some with you in this can."

I went back inside and packed my toys. A wooden top from Pepé and a wooden knife that my uncle made for me. I was ready. The tracks ran by our home, close enough that the house would shake when the train came through town twice a day. I had always dreamed of taking that train. And now I would take that train to where the pine forests grew.

But when we left two days later, we did not board a train. Pepé had made a cabinet for a pilot and he gave us seats on the mail plane. In the 1950's the mail was delivered by air but there weren't enough passengers to fill all the seats. As we stepped out on the tarmac for the first leg of our flight, the plane looked small to me. There was an engine and a propeller on each wing. It's nose pointed almost straight up when it was sitting on the ground. My sister Helen and I got to sit by a window. When the engine started the plane began to vibrate terribly, but the flight attendant must have seen my concern and smiled at me. As we roared down the runway, I did my part and pulled up hard on the armrests to help the plane get up in the air.

After we were in the air, the same stewardess came back and brought us silverware and white cloth napkins before bringing us a meal. I lost track and don't remember how many mail stops we made, but we spent the night on the plane before we got off in San Francisco late the next day. My uncle had flown out before us and somehow we all packed into his 1948 Buick for the long drive to Klamath Falls, Oregon.

Pepé had found a large ranch, with a main house and even a bunkhouse big enough for everyone, grandparents, aunts and uncles, and my three cousins. I played more with my cousins than my younger sister Helen. But my father couldn't find a job in Klamath Falls and took a job at a small mill in Canby. It was seventy miles away and too far for our old car to make that trip everyday. So we moved to Canby, a small town on the California side of the border. I was just in time to start first grade.

We moved into a two-room shack with an attic where the kids slept. In the winter, the snow got so high we had to go into our house through the attic window. The kitchen was the only source of heat. On Saturday my mother filled a wash tub half full of snow and then added hot water until the temperature was just right. My dad would take the first bath, then my older brother and me, then my little brother and little sister, always in that order. My mother took her bath late at night after everyone else was done. That was when she also bathed our new baby sister. After our bath we would stand by the oven door to dry off. Sometimes, when my mother was busy with the baby, my brother and I would sneak out the back door and jump in the snow naked. This was so we could stand near the oven door to warm up again.

In the spring, the snow geese returned from the south and landed in the field next to the house. My sister and I tried to sneak up on them, but we could never get very close. On one of his visits, Pepé told us that we had to be in the field before the geese landed and he helped us a dig a shallow hole in the snow big enough for my sister and me to lie down in. He covered us with a sheet and put a piece of sagebrush on top. After we were settled he said, "When I was a boy, we would lie still and when the geese landed I would grab one by the leg. I still remember the taste of wild goose."

We almost froze before the geese landed. But sure enough, one of them came close. I grabbed the goose by the leg and held on. Pepé forgot to mention that those geese could bite hard and beat us with their wings. But we held on and made it into the house and said, "Pepé, here is a goose for you to take home and cook."

As the goose beat me over the head with its wings, Pepé said, "I am really proud of you, but I have food in the cupboard. It would be wrong to kill a goose when we don't need food. Let it go and it will return someday when our hunger is great."

Pepé opened the door and the goose shot off as if it had been fired from a cannon. Our first summer there we learned that the well went dry. My father built a hand pump to bring up water in the dry time. But in the summer there were rattlesnakes on the path to the pump. He solved that problem by building a boardwalk out to the pump. He was so happy with his work that he built another boardwalk to the outhouse. Besides keeping our feet dry, the boardwalk turned out to be popular with the rattlesnakes. It would be over a hundred degrees in the summer and the rattlesnakes would come to cool off in the shade under the boardwalks. They would rattle and strike at the sound of our footsteps. My sister Helen and I would lie on the boardwalk and poke sticks at the snakes just to hear them rattle and hit the boards.

That would drive my mother crazy, but it was safer than when we left the boardwalk to climb up the hill behind the house and hunt for arrowheads. I was five and Helen was only four, but we would roll some bread and peanut butter in a blanket and make camp beneath a tree. Most often my mother and father wouldn't notice that we had gone. Their habit of drinking left us a lot of freedom to come and go.

But as things seemed to happen, my father's job at the mill ran out and we packed up again. The family moved to Seattle, but this time I didn't move with them. Pepé insisted that I stay with him and Memé at the ranch in Klamath Falls.

TWO

I WANTED TO GO WITH MY FAMILY and I was sad that they left me. But I settled in with Pepé and Memé. Pepé was a medicine man and spiritual leader. People came to him for herbs and plants to heal their different ailments. I would join Pepé when he went out to collect herbs for his medicine bundle. We spent days camping in the desert collecting different herbs and plants. As we sat by the campfire, he would tell me, "Everything from the ground, everything that happens to us in life is a gift from the Creator."

He took me on his frequent travels to South Dakota to visit Frank Fools Crow, a renowned spiritual leader of the Oglala Sioux. They talked very little, but would sit for hours, absorbing life around them. On one of our trips, we went to do a Sun Dance to honor the Creator and perhaps be given visions. The government feared the power of the Sun Dance and it was against the law at that time. We walked all day into the Black Hills until we reached a secret spot. The young men had built a sweat lodge and were waiting for my grandfather and Frank Fools Crow to lead them in the purification ceremony before the Sun Dance. Many men were milling about. I was only eight and I was shy.

Frank Fools Crow came over to where I was half hiding in the brush and invited me to enter the purification sweat lodge. I wanted to say, "No." But Pepé nodded his head and signaled for me to say, "Yes." When the stones in the fire were hot, all the men began to undress. I followed them with my underwear still on. Frank Fools Crow leaned over and said that all the guys would think something was wrong with my penis if I kept them on. Sheepishly, I took my underwear off and kept my hands over my genitals as if to protect them from disappearing. Somehow, I made it through all four rounds of the sweat lodge. My chest almost burst with pride.

Pepé told the story over and over to my uncles and they all laughed, but he always ended the story by saying that he was so proud of me. We stayed and watched the Sun Dance. The men were brave and endured. After the celebration, I was chosen to offer water to the dancers, a huge honor not often given to children. I was happy that I made my grandfather proud.

I knew that Frank Fool's Crow was a famous spiritual leader, but I was surprised that he and his wife lived in a broken down tarpaper shack. Frank Fools Crow and Pepé always talked about the Creator and it seemed to me that the Creator should get Frank Fools Crow and his wife a better house. I never said that out loud, but I think Frank Fools Crow could read minds and one day when I was looking at his shack he smiled and said, "The Creator has given me everything I need. I don't need a fancy house and a lot of things that I would never use. We share all the gifts from the Creator. After all, the Creator gives them freely to us."

There was no grass in Frank Fools Crow's front yard. It was way too dry for that. There was a weathered gray picnic table, a couple of old wooden chairs and a Chevy pickup with four flat tires. Across from the pickup was a skeleton of a willow sweat lodge and a fire pit. From there a path went to the outhouse and over to the hand pump. Pepé and I cleared an area of stones and debris so that we would have a flat spot on which to sleep. On many of the hot summer nights, Pepé and I slept outside in Frank Fools Crow's front yard. We slept on beds of fresh sagebrush and hay.

Frank Fools Crow was always up before dawn and would bring in a bucket of water to Mrs. Frank. His first wife died of a stroke and I asked, "Could you have saved her life with your medicine?"

He smiled and said, "There are some things that shouldn't be asked for, no matter how much you want them."

He picked up a small, black, round, smooth stone with white specks and closed his hand around it. He closed his eyes and bowed his head. His breathing slowed. After several minutes, he handed the stone to me. It was hot, but I didn't drop it. I closed my fist. He stared into my eyes and said, "Become the stone. Stone medicine is very powerful. The stones know the ancient ways. Becoming the stone will teach you many important things."

Each morning Frank Fools Crow and Pepé spread out their blankets and opened their medicine bundles to greet the Creator, the Ancestors, the Sun and Mother Earth. They would softly sing their personal songs that had been given to them as young men on their first vision quest. I didn't have a personal song, but Pepé gave me a song that came from his father. He said "Sing it with pride. Songs are the first communications between babies and the Ancestors. Babies sing long before they talk. Songs are our most cherished gifts."

We would sit on the blankets as the sun came up over the hills to the east. They would light some sage and sweet grass in large flat shells. The smoke would drift up and fill the air with the smell of the desert and the mountains and bring the Creator to the ceremony. On those cold mornings, I would sit very still and let the sun warm my bare chest and face and take away the goose bumps. Pepé and Frank Fools Crow would stop singing and sit with their hands in their laps, palms facing up to receive any gifts from the Creator. They held their heads high and closed their eyes as they took deep breaths in unison.

After the morning greetings, Mrs. Frank always had some hot cereal for us sweetened with butter and raspberry jam with a pot of strong black tea. We ate outside. Everyday was the same and I was surprised when one morning, Frank Fools Crow told us, "Today will be special. We are going to dedicate the new gym at the tribal center. In the days ahead, there will be many celebrations in that building. There will be many people coming and spiritual leaders visiting from all four directions."

It turns out that Pepé and Frank Fools Crow were to be the lead spiritual leaders. The dedication would take place that morning and there would be a powwow with food, dancing, drumming and singing at noon. We piled into Pepé's pickup. I sat between Frank

Fools Crow and Mrs. Frank. She smelled of wood smoke and Ivory soap. I fell asleep but she nudged me when we were almost to the gym. It was going to be named for Red Shirt, one of the chiefs who was at the battle of the Little Big Horn. It started to rain, a hard rain with thunder and lightning. Cars and trucks spun their wheels in the mud. No one could move on the road. No one could reach the gym.

I walked through the muck to a small knoll with Frank Fools Crow and Pepé. The two old spiritual leaders stood in the rain with bared chests, their arms held up and sang songs to the Creator. They asked for the rain to go away and the sun to come out. After thirty minutes the rain stopped and the sun came out. I stood beside Pepé. I didn't know the songs Frank Fools Crow sang, nor did I understand his language. The celebration in the gym went on for six hours until a boy came out of the gym and told us that the celebration was over. Pepé and Frank Fools Crow lowered their arms and we slowly walked back to the pickup. As we drove away, the clouds closed in. The sky opened up and the rain came down. It rained for two days and nights.

The time that I spent with my grandfather and Frank Fools Crow was a turning point in my life. I was raised Catholic but I listened when Frank Fools Crow said, "I see the Creator in all things around me. There is a spirit in everything I can see and touch, right down to the finest grain of sand. I thank the Creator for the beauty of the sunrise and the sunset."

I couldn't put those thoughts into words then, but I began to see that we are related to all things. I started to become more attentive to gifts and my place on this earth and began to understand what Pepé and Frank Fools Crow meant when they said, "Everything is a gift."

THREE

THE MONTHS PASSED INTO YEARS WHEN, one day, shortly before my tenth birthday, Pepé told me "It is time for you to go back home to your family. I have nothing more to teach you of the old ways."

By then, his home was my home. I wanted to stay but a few days later I packed my clothes and the medicine bundle that Pepé helped me make. My mother and father and three of my brothers and sisters came to pick me up. My older brother was away in the seminary. I hadn't used English for so long that it was hard to answer everyone's questions. It was a ten-hour ride to Seattle, but it felt much longer than that. I was angry and hurt that my grandparents didn't want me and I had a hard time understanding my family's conversations.

At my grandparents' home, I had spent most of the time outside, but I learned that was not how people in Seattle lived. My family lived in an old four-story boarding house on Capital Hill. A long winding stairway led to each floor. At each landing there was a large bay window with a bench seat. The hall smelled of old wood, mildew and cooking smells from the different apartments. I would sit on the bench on the top floor and watch the Kalakala Ferry go back and forth across Puget Sound.

My mother enrolled me at St. Teresa's Catholic School. Though I was a lot bigger and older than the other kids, I had forgotten most of my English and I was put in the first grade. My grandparents had at one point been devout Catholics, but before I lived with them they reverted to practicing their Native American beliefs and had left the Catholic Church. St. Teresa's was not a good fit for me.

I used to read to Memé every night and I was up to a fourth grade level, but speaking English was another story. Even when I read I would translate into the trade dialect that my grandparents used. Sometimes, I would get confused and mixed up. One day when it was my turn at reading time, I read the English words, but spoke them out loud in the trade dialect. The nun was livid and said, "Stop speaking that nonsense."

She rapped my knuckles with a ruler. My hands stung and the embarrassment hurt me deep inside. Without thinking, I snatched the ruler out of her hand. She grabbed the ruler back and struck me again. Then pulling me by my ear, she marched me on my tiptoes toward the door. Somehow, I was able to break free. I ran and jumped out the second story window. The second before I hit the pavement I tucked myself into a ball. Pepé would have said that the Creator rolled me in a ball to spare me any broken bones. In any case, I got up and ran straight home. That evening two nuns came to the door to formally expel me from St. Teresa. After they left my mother said, "That's just as well. You might have gotten hurt on your next jump."

I didn't like school anyway, but I wondered what I would do. But they never enrolled me in another school in Seattle. My parents had just found a house near the Muckleshoot reservation in Auburn. My father's first cousin Tut had married a woman from the Muckleshoot tribe and I would have cousins to play with. That was all I needed to hear. In Auburn, I was placed in fourth grade, much closer to kids my own age. I was given a lot of after school help and it wasn't long before I caught up with the rest of the class.

I began to like school then and in fact it was better than home. My parents were often gone on long drinking spells and finally we were taken and put into foster homes. But it was always back and forth. When we came home, Grandma Squires, my mother's mother who lived with us in the bigger house, was always there for us. Grandma Squires was on relief and didn't have much money. But when the State Fair in Puyallup came around she always had saved something for the kids. Back then, the fair was a big deal. School closed for the day. The teachers even gave us free tickets because the fair exhibits were considered educational. That could have been true, but it's safe to say that we went to more food booths and took in more rides than science exhibits.

We rode on the last steam driven train on the west coast, from Auburn to Puyallup and got off near the fair grounds. Though money was tight, somehow Grandma Squires always had five dollars for each of us four kids. With money in my pocket, I would head off for the roller coaster. The tickets were fifty cents each and I would buy five dollars worth. When lines for the rides got really long, I would sell tickets to the kids who were near the end of the line for a dollar each. I always had enough to pay Grandma Squires back and even stop at the Fisher Flour Scone booth. I would purchase six scones with raspberry jam to take home to grandma. But on the train ride home, they looked so good that, in the end, I only had three or four to give her.

Sometimes, we would be in a foster home for a few weeks. We would come back home and then we would end up in the foster home again. But when we were home, I was the oldest and so I learned to cook and run the washing machine. I made sure my younger sisters and brother were fed and got to school on time.

When we needed money for milk and school lunches my cousin Tut would give it to us – that is, if he was not off drinking with my parents. But if he was drinking too, Tut's wife would always help. We called her Auntie and Tut, though he was my cousin, was Uncle. Back then, out of respect, we called older people Aunt and Uncle. I liked Auburn better than Seattle, but the next year my dad found another job and we moved again.

FOUR

MY FATHER WAS HIRED to install a planer in the lumber mill in Curlew, Washington. Located in the Cascade Mountain Range, only fifteen miles south of the Canadian border, Curlew was a far cry from Seattle or even from our last stop in Auburn. Curlew had a population of only a few hundred people. There was a general store with a post office in the back. Besides that there was a restaurant, a gas station and a tavern where my father could be found when he wasn't at the mill.

But for me Curlew was perfect. There was a lot of country to explore. All the kids in town had .22 rifles and we hunted and camped out on weekends. During the summer, when we weren't putting up hay, we'd camp along the river, or in the hills along a stream, where we could fish and hunt grouse. We lived off the land, if only for the weekend. On one of our camp outs, my brother and I found a porcupine's den with three kittens in it. We stuck around the den for the better part of two days, but the mother never came back. Maybe she was killed by a cougar while she was out looking for food.

Two of the kittens died and I took the surviving one home. My mother let me keep it and gave me a bottle of warm milk to feed it with. I named him "Six" which is the name for friend in the trade language that my grandparents spoke. Six liked to sleep in my bed, but with his quills, I had to be careful not to kick him or roll on him. There are no quills on a porcupine's belly and he loved me to rub his stomach or scratch under his chin.

Porcupines bark like a small dog. They are vegetarians and in the wild, they eat lots of tree bark. Six really loved fruit and at our house, that's mostly what he ate. He became part of the family. He'd be with us all day, but being nocturnal by nature, he would leave at night. But he always came back each morning. When he didn't come home one morning, I was worried. Sure enough, on the way to school, I found Six along the side of the road where he had been hit by a car.

I recognized his collar. Whenever there was a party going on at the community hall across the street I used to attach a leash to it. Otherwise Six would go over to the party and beg for food and beer. Six had a taste for beer. He walked down to the tavern every evening. He was a favorite there and they would set a saucer of beer on the floor for him. There was only one customer who didn't like the idea of a porcupine in the tavern. Once, just once, he tried to boot Six out. He learned his lesson when Six flipped his tail at him and left some quills in his boot. But in the end, it was Six's fondness for beer that led him to walk unsteadily out onto the highway. It was like losing my best friend.

But it wasn't long after Six's demise that a log truck driver, knowing how badly we felt, brought us a fawn whose mother had been killed. My mother would mix some powdered calf formula and put it in a bottle. The fawn, a little buck that we named Dandy, took right to it. In fact, he seemed to get bigger every day. Soon, he was jumping the low fence around the yard. That was in the spring and he settled into the gazebo in our yard. My six-year-old brother, Paul, and I moved our beds out there and we called it our summer house. When the fall weather turned, we moved back into the house where Dandy wandered around like he owned it. When my mother was cooking dinner or canning vegetables he would sniff the pot to see what was cooking. He would graze in the garden and leave us almost nothing to harvest. He ate all our houseplants. My mother drew the line at dinnertime. When he would beg for food, she would kick him out of the house.

By his second year, Dandy was an impressive buck and he looked quite striking in the bright red collar that my mother made for him. The locals knew him by that collar and during the hunting season I also put a bell on him to warn hunters that he was nearby. But in his second year, during the rut, Dandy took off looking for a girlfriend. All the local hunters knew Dandy, but one evening in the tavern, a hunter from Seattle was bragging about the deer he had bagged. When he said, "This stupid buck practically walked right up to me..." my father left the tavern and looked in the back of the pickup. Dandy still had his collar on. He took the collar into the tavern and asked the hunter, "Are you the owner of the blue pickup with the deer in back?"

The hunter slid off his stool and proudly said, "I bagged it just two hours ago!"

My father was a hunter too, but he set Dandy's collar on the counter and punched him in the jaw. He kept on swinging and it took a bunch of the regulars to pull my father off. Even so, the man had to go to the hospital for stitches before he left town. Dandy was the last animal that we took in. A few years later, the mill owners tried to bring in some non-union labor and the mill mysteriously burned to the ground. We moved back to the other side of the mountains to the town of Pacific near the Muckleshoot reservation.

Our family settled in, but my father wasn't home much. He traveled all over the states, Canada and even South America to install planers in the lumber mills. He always brought some presents when he came back, but it was a relief when he left. By then his drinking was worse and he was mean when he was drinking. We tried to stay out of his way, but the lumber industry slowed down and my father was around more and more. He and my mother both drank a lot and my brothers and sisters and I were in and out of foster homes. But the system always gave my parents another chance.

The neighbors would hear my parents fight and call the police. When the welfare people began checking in more often, my father decided it was time to move again. This time, we moved near a town called Black Diamond on the east end of the Muckleshoot Reservation. Somehow my father bought some property and brought in a mobile home. It seemed like we were miles from nowhere and things got even worse.

Music saved my life. Years earlier, when I was only three, my older brother and I found a violin in the attic of Grandma Squire's home. She hadn't played it for years and for the most part it remained in it's case until I started taking lessons. In high school, I used practicing as a way to stay after school and then go to my favorite foster home and ask to spend the night. If only to get away from home, I practiced and practiced. My foster mother was an excellent piano player and she would accompany me for my challenges in music at the state contest that were held once a year.

In my senior year, I put together a tape and in January, 1964, I submitted it to Western Washington Teachers College in Bellingham for a scholarship. That was the only way I could have gone to college. I waited and waited. I heard nothing and finally, in August of that year, I moved to Grandma Squire's home in Orange, Massachusetts. She had returned there a few years earlier. Grandma Squires read in the local newspaper about a state nursing program and encouraged me to apply. I was accepted and I headed to Gardner State Hospital. For two years, I worked at the hospital in the morning and took classes in the afternoon. We were given a stipend of twenty dollars a week and a room to live in. But I still hoped to do the music program that I applied for. Years later I found out that I was accepted to the program with a full scholarship but the mail went to my parents and they never told me. To this day, I don't understand why. Did they not want me to go? Were their own lives so scattered that they lost it or was there another reason?

I finished the nursing program and became a psychiatric nurse. But I got homesick and returned to Washington to get my nursing license. By then, my father and mother were divorced. I took a job in the local hospital and helped Mom make payments on the mobile home and helped to take care of the youngest kids who were still in school. My mother was dating a retired Army Sergeant who worked with her at the Boeing Aircraft plant.

When they got married, no one said anything, but it felt like it was time for me to leave. I didn't see many options in front of me. At the end of 1967, I joined the Navy and headed to boot camp in San Diego.

FIVE

Down at the induction center at pier 91 on the Seattle waterfront, there were maybe thirty of us standing around naked. Embarrassed, we just looked down at our feet until someone yelled, "Line up single file. Spit out your gum. Put your papers in your right hand. There will be no talking."

In short order we had to cough for a hernia check, bend over for a rectal and take a short exam for hearing and vision. Feeling like a cow being led to slaughter, I was envious of the men whose forms were stamped 4-F and rejected on the spot for poor vision or flat feet. After we dressed, those of us who were unfortunate enough to pass the physical were bused from pier 91 to the airport in SeaTac, fifteen miles away. Along with guys from Oklahoma, Georgia, Arkansas, Texas and every part of the country, I boarded a plane and we flew toward the Navy boot camp in San Diego. Most of us weren't too excited except for my neighbor, a tall blond man who not only looked like Gomer Pyle, but talked like him too. After the plane took off, he asked "Can I switch seats with you so I can look out the window?"

After we traded seats, I tried to get some sleep, but he kept talking. "Look at all them lights. When I left Arkansas, my mama told me she was going to leave the porch light on and I could wave to her."

Before I finally drifted off to sleep, he said, "Sure enough. My mama kept her word. I can see the porch light on!"

I thought to myself, he could do an ad for Motel 6, the one that says, "We'll leave the light on for you." But I didn't say anything and he continued, "Sure makes a guy feel good to know his mama left the porch light on for him."

Boot camp wasn't as bad as I thought it would be. Every morning we had to line up in our underwear at the foot of our bunks and stand at attention until the drill instructor inspected our lockers and our bunks. It was the biggest waste of time, but I didn't mind the daily exercises afterwards. They kept us busy and graduation day from boot camp came up quickly. For the most part, we dispersed to other parts of the country, but my bunkmate, Steve, and I were both assigned to Corps School at the Naval Hospital in San Diego.

I was already a registered psychiatric nurse and Corps School was boring as hell. It was the same for Steve who had worked with a veterinarian all through high school. So during the three-month program, the two of us spent a lot of days at the San Diego Zoo and Balboa Park. If we wore our uniform we could get into the park and zoo for free. The park had a great archery range and we would often spend a full day at the range. During those three months as we prepared for the deployment, I became pretty good with a bow and arrow.

Finally, Steve and I, along with eight or ten of the guys from Corps School got our orders to ship out to Guam. It wasn't a given, but I knew that my next stop after Guam could be Vietnam. I hadn't been to church for ten or fifteen years, but young men were dying every day in the war. I thought maybe it would be good to cover all my bases. I went to the cathedral in San Diego for confession. I told the priest, "I don't know where to start. It has been at least ten years since my last confession."

He responded, "Since it's been so long, you will need to say five rosaries."

"Jesus Christ. I didn't kill anybody."

Without batting an eye, he said, "Now it will be six!"

With fifteen days of leave before we shipped out, most of the corpsman went home to visit their families. Would my family have time to visit with me or would they be too caught up in the constant chaos and crises that defined their lives? Growing up, strange as it might have been, everything seemed normal. It was just what it was. Funny what time and distance can do. I loved them, but for the first time, I began to see that my family was anything but normal.

I jumped at the chance to go to Montana with Steve, not just because Montana was supposed to be beautiful, but also because Steve's parents were "normal." They sounded like the Cleavers on the TV show *Leave It To Beaver*. They were the family I needed to spend time with before going to war. I spent a week hiking and fishing the lakes and streams in Glacier National Park with Steve and his parents. Outside of the park, we even tried to do a little hunting. We drove up to a highland lake where Steve's dad spotted a large blue grouse sitting right by the road. There were rifles and shotguns in the truck, but Steve pulled out a bow. I grabbed the quiver of arrows and said, "What the hell do you think you're doing? I'm the Indian in this group!"

Steve shrugged and handed me the bow. I drew the arrow back and let it fly. I was way off the mark. The grouse had no respect for my heritage and didn't even flinch. Steve picked up a rock the size of a golf ball. He wound up as if he were pitching a baseball. The rock struck the bird in the head. The bird flipped over and didn't move. Steve shook his head and said, "No wonder the Indians lost so many wars."

I had to say, "Now just a minute. Don't forget Custer!"

Steve and I have played the Indian/White thing ever since. But mostly we just fished along the Kootenai River. We had trout for breakfast every morning and Steve's parents put a lot in their freezer. Part of me just wanted to stay fishing and camping with Steve and his family, but I headed to the Muckleshoot Reservation where my mother was living. Things were never easy in our family, but my mother had a job at the Boeing plant and was married to Sarge, my new stepfather.

But even what should have been good news, wasn't. My baby sister Renette was living with them and I could see that something wasn't right. Renette was afraid of Sarge. My father had abused my older sister and I wasn't going to take any chances. I arranged for Renette to move in with a boot camp friend's family in South Bend.

As soon as Renette got settled and enrolled in school, I caught a plane to San Francisco, the first leg of a flight to Anderson Air Force

Base for duty at Guam Naval Hospital. Steve was on the same flight and after we landed we stowed our gear in an old WWII barracks. Only now, the wounded were coming from the fighting in Vietnam and casualties arrived daily. On our days off, we went snorkeling in the bomb craters left from the WWII invasion. The highlight was a hike into the beautiful Telifofo Falls to go skinny-dipping. And sometimes the scenery was enhanced by some stewardesses who were swimming there too.

It was true what they said about military chow. "The food tastes terrible and there was never enough."

Fortunately, right across the road from the barracks there was a small café, a hut really. We could get a bowl of saimin soup that consisted of oriental noodles in a chicken broth topped with a cut-up boiled egg, chopped green onion, and a small amount of barbecue pork. The soup was great and Rosie was friendly and eager to hear about the United States. Rosie invited us to the local fiestas that took place in the small villages throughout the island. The beer at the base was really cheap so Steve and I would bring that to share and the locals would ply us with food. My favorite dish from those feasts is called Kelaguen. It's made with shredded coconut, lime, water, peeled shrimp and the hot peppers that grow on the island. We needed the cold beer to cut through the heat of those peppers.

Liquor was also cheap at the PX, only nine dollars for a bottle of Scotch. On payday, Steve and I would buy a bottle and go to the outdoor community movie. We had to sit with our feet off the ground away from the rabies-infested shrews that roamed the island. It was hard to keep my feet up after drinking Jack Daniels. I got bit by a shrew one night and had to get a series of rabies shots. The treatment consisted of seven shots on each side of my stomach and hurt like hell. After that, there were no more movies for me and my outings off the base were only to the market. Vendors sold all kinds of tropical fruit and vegetables along with handmade baskets and mats that were woven from palm fronds.

I also discovered the betel nut at the market. It is a round brownish nut about the size of a large grape that the locals chewed. It turns your teeth and the inside of your mouth a dark, almost black red color. It also gives you a feeling of well being, a mellow feeling that life is okay. It also takes away your appetite. I lost the thirty pounds I gained eating the fiesta food on Guam. It was maybe not the best weight loss program, but when we shipped out to Vietnam a year and a half later, I was back to my induction weight.

Being stationed on Guam was a safe place during the war, but there were still some dangers lurking. We sometimes encountered old bullets and hand grenades left over from World War II. We would report our finds and a team of specialists would come and remove the live artillery from the beach or reef. They had a dangerous task. On the south side of the island, a team of demolition experts worked to disarm a mine. It was a Pineapple mine, one of the large round objects with a lot of pins protruding from it. Sadly, the mine exploded and killed two men and wounded the other two members of the team.

When we got to Vietnam, we had to deal with the casualties from the land mines called Bouncing Bettys. When a soldier stepped on the mine and triggered it, the mine would bounce up about waist high and explode. The mines would be filled with nails and screws and sometimes with human feces to cause infection in the victim. Caring for abdominal, chest, and head wounds was a daily business on the hospital ship. Casualties came in day and night and sometimes we would be in surgery for seventy-two hours. They delivered food to the recovery room so that we could keep going.

We had to deal with a lot of head wounds. When we were notified that a GI was down with a severe head wound, our neurosurgeon would get the hospital to call in a chopper that took me to the battlefield to start the initial care. The surgeon was an egomaniac, but his care plan from the battlefront to the recovery room saved a lot of lives. Most of my tour of duty was on that hospital ship. On one of my last times on the beach, I was wounded. After being patched up, I spent an extended six months on the ship and began working with an anesthesiologist who taught me how to do this delicate procedure. Before I was sent home, my plan was to become a nurse anesthesiologist. But even though the chief surgeon warned me it's possible to lose someone from their injures while we administered the anesthetic, when it happened to me, I knew I couldn't face that event again.

While I stayed on the hospital ship, Steve was stationed with the Third Marines near Danang. I would visit him in Danang once in a while. On one of those visits we had been out drinking and were sleeping soundly when rocket fire hit the compound. We sat bolt upright. It wasn't a direct hit, but one of the rockets was close enough that it shook the barracks we were sleeping in. We grabbed some clothes and headed for the bunker. More rockets were coming in. Mud was flying everywhere and by the time we got to the bunker we were *mudded* from head to toe. In the dim light, looking at Steve, all I could see was the whites of his eyes. As it turned out this was the last time I would see Steve for forty years.

On ship I befriended a guy named Carl. At a time when few gay men acknowledged it, he admitted to several of us that he was gay. That was probably not a good thing. He was shunned by almost everyone on board ship. He was beaten up several times, but didn't report it out of fear of retaliation and of being dishonorably discharged. He was an excellent corpsman though and I offered him a position in the recovery room mostly to keep him away from the thugs that bothered some sailors. I didn't care and didn't pay attention to what those people thought. Maybe I should have.

When our ship was in dry dock at Subic Bay in the Philippines I was approached by a First Class Petty Officer who did his Commander's bidding and invited me to come to the Commander's quarters for a drink later that evening. "It's just a chance to talk about the Recovery Room and Surgery. No big deal, but a little less formal."

Later that evening, the same First Class Petty Officer answered the door. As he said, it did seem pretty relaxed, but I wasn't real comfortable. I had a drink in hand when the Commander asked, "What do you know about the other corpsmen that are under your supervision?"

His tone made me defensive, but I said, "Everyone that works in the recovery room is at least Third Class and has prior experience. We deal with some serious wounds."

Seeming to ignore what I said, the Commander asked, "Do you know that you have a guy working in the recovery room who is a queer?"

Not sure what to say, I sipped my drink but didn't respond. The commander went on: "It's illegal and he should be court martialed out of the Navy with a bad conduct discharge. Do you know what those queers do to each other for sex?"

I put my drink down and got up to leave, but the door was blocked and the Commander said, "It was your job to report it. You will have to be punished."

The First Class goon removed his dungarees. I begged them to let me out, but the Commander and the First Class took turns using me for a punching bag. Then they grabbed me and laughed and said, "We'll show you what your friend Carl does."

To this day, it's hard to say it, but they beat me and raped me. Then they said, "This will teach you to protect queers. Now get the hell out. You tell anyone and you'll be shark bait."

I did tell Carl though. He wanted to report it to the commanding officer of the ship. But I told him, "Who will believe me over the Lt. Commander and his goon who are career Navy?" Carl said, "Let's go back to the ship and kill the bastards."

I shook my head and said, "I don't want to go to prison for these bastards. Someday, they'll get what's coming to them. It's the way things work out."

Once on the plane going stateside, I relaxed a little, but I spent the last six months in the service looking over my shoulder. Years later I have had patients and clients confide in me about abuse that happened to them. As horrible as it was for me, my experience helped me understand their anger, grief and trauma. As Pepé used to say, "Everything is a Gift."

SIX

I REMEMBER CLEARLY HOW IT WAS before I boarded the plane and said goodbye to Vietnam. I know I am retracing my steps here, but I believe it's necessary. You don't just fly, fly away home. In reality you live and re-live what you lived. You find yourself haunted by what happened, by what you left behind. I have talked to some vets who said they actually missed Vietnam. They missed who they'd come to love, both their comrades, their bunkmates, their burdens, even their nightmares. As I flew home I saw green, I saw red, I saw the sea, and even though I was leaving, I was also returning, like a dream that curves in space and keeps bringing you back.

There was so much sadness in Vietnam, but we were soldiers and we had our mission. To get up each morning and face the day, we had to wall off our feelings. I tried, but I remember when the sadness, like a wave, came over that wall and overwhelmed me.

I looked down at the sandwich in my hand. Blood from a wounded GI was splattered all over the bread. I didn't question which GI's blood was on my sandwich, but I lifted up the top piece of bread and tried to identify the slice of meat beneath some wilted lettuce. The meat was smeared with so much congealed mayonnaise that I couldn't even try to guess. It was another mystery meat sandwich. I shrugged and took a bite. It didn't matter anyway. The food had no taste. It was only fuel so I could keep going.

Since we couldn't leave the operating theater, the galley would send up some food to keep us going. As soon as one chopper headed off for the battlefront to rescue more wounded another chopper would land on the deck. We had been in surgery for two days and two nights with only ten minute breaks every couple of hours. Sometimes, we would be in surgery for seventy-two hours straight. One day would blend into the next. At the same time, the doctors, nurses and corpsman I worked with were professionals. We did our best to save each soldier.

The first time that I pulled off a young soldier's boot, his foot came with it, and my stomach did flip-flops. I took my sandwich and threw it in the garbage where it belonged. Several hours later, I was weak from hunger and learned my lesson the hard way. Food is fuel. After that, I always ate my sandwich and good thing I did, because once a soldier came in with a gaping hole in his chest near the artery to his heart. The hole was big enough for me to put most of my hand in the wound and apply pressure to the artery that was squirting blood. But I knew that if I removed my hand, he would bleed to death. I could feel his heart pulsing on my fingertips. Surgery was backed up and they told me to just keep applying pressure. Easy for them to say. I don't know how long it took before a surgeon could operate. During that time, the best I could do was to take a few sips of water. By then, I was beyond exhaustion, but his heart kept beating. He made it and with a wound like that he earned a ticket home.

Some days, I wasn't sure if I could keep going. Sometimes, the never ending flow of wounded soldiers felt overwhelming, but then I only had to look around and see the other corpsman, nurses and surgeons at work. There was no quit in them. Commander Easter, or "mom" as we called her was almost always by my side when we delivered anesthesia. Mom was one of the kindest people on this earth. She told me, "When I leave the Navy, I will never give another anesthesia. I am going to open a hot dog stand close to Madigan Army Hospital and give away free hot dogs to any GI that stops by."

Commander Peg Burrell was the nurse in charge of the recovery room. She spoke with a strong Boston accent. Barely five feet tall, she had enough spunk that left no doubt she was in charge. Yet, she could handle the most difficult patients with kindness and caring. I told myself if they can keep working, I could too. The amputations were wrenching, but I think the head wounds were the hardest for me. Most of those who came in with head wounds were not going to survive. Head wounds were the hardest to care for. Fevers would spike and temperatures would often go up to one hundred and five or one hundred and six degrees Fahrenheit and would destroy what was left of their brain. As if the odds for those poor soldiers weren't bad enough, at one point, the hypothermic cooling mattress broke and the replacement was back ordered. Out of desperation we made a cooling mattress with a washing machine to cycle cold water through the mattress. It was crude. It was ugly, but it saved lives.

When we operated on kids from the orphanage it gave me a good feeling to be able to help them. We did a lot of surgeries to repair cleft palates. Before the United States was involved in the war, Vietnam had been a French colony. Vietnam remained a rice-growing nation, but the French liked polished rice instead of whole grain rice. Rice is a major part of the Vietnamese diet and though polished rice suited the French palate, it did not provide as many nutrients as whole grain rice. The deficiencies in their new diet led to a high incidence of Vietnamese children born with cleft palates.

Our primary goal was to care for our wounded. If there was no incoming we might have a break. We couldn't leave the ship, but we could go up on the deck and sit in the sun or shoot some hoops at the makeshift basketball court. But we could never relax, because as soon as we did, we would hear the choppers coming in. Sometimes, I would leave the ship, but that was no holiday either. In fact, it was more like going from the frying pan into the fire.

Because I was a corpsman, sometimes I would go with the neurosurgeon to pick up GIs with head wounds. He liked to begin the care for head wounds out in the field. Then we would transport the wounded soldiers to the hospital ship. At anytime, I could be given notice to board a chopper in ten minutes. When that happened I would grab my medical bag. It was mostly full of bandages, pressures dressings, morphine and syringes. That was all I could take. The bag had to be light and only weighed about ten pounds. I just took the clothes on my back and would grab my poncho. I might be at the battlefield for just an hour or two, but if we were pinned down by heavy fire a rescue chopper might not get back for a day or two. I could use my poncho for protection from the rain and roll up in it at night and use it as a blanket. In that case, my medical bag would serve double duty as a pillow. I traveled light, but with all the comforts of home.

Depending on our destination the flight might take thirty minutes to an hour. As we got close, I would make sure my corpsman insignia or the Red Cross insignia was not on my uniform. The snipers liked to take out the corpsman to demoralize the company. I would grab my bag and ready myself to jump as soon as we got close to the ground. A helicopter is a big target so the gunner would be set up with an automatic gun on a tripod to provide some firepower and cover when the door opened. I always tried to hit the ground running, but I also had to crouch down. Too many people have gotten injured or killed by those blades. The chopper would lift off as quickly as it could, so even after touching down the blades never stopped spinning. Straw and dirt would fly through the air. It made me less of a target, but at the same time I could hardly see for the first hundred feet.

I had to quickly sort out how many casualties there were and try to have them ready for the next chopper that would be coming in. A chopper was limited in the number of casualties it could carry in addition to the crew. Sometimes they carried ten or twelve casualties and sometimes only three. The remaining casualties would have to wait to see if they could get on the next chopper. It could be a long wait. Sometimes the worst happened. A helicopter would get hit and then blow up as it was touching down or departing. I was onboard ship when the First Marines took a huge hit during the Tet Offensive in 1968. They lost almost an entire company in what turned out to be one of the biggest losses of the war. I helped care for a lot of survivors during that time.

If I came in to replace a corpsman who had completed his tour, I'd then fill in with his patrol for a week. I knew what to expect, but it was a dangerous transition for a new, inexperienced corpsman. The Viet Cong were quite sophisticated and in the night one of them might call out, "Corpsman."

Our first instinct would be to head over to help a wounded

soldier, but we would be walking into a deadly trap. A new corpsman was more likely to be fooled, because even with training, things were different on the ground. There was a learning curve, but since we just replaced a corpsman that was rotating out there was no corpsman on site to be a mentor. The logistics looked good on paper but there was no unit cohesion. I'm sure the casualty rate for inexperienced corpsman was higher in a system like that. But after making it through my first couple of patrols I had more confidence.

It was miserable slogging through the jungle in the heat and the humidity, but even though we always had to be alert during the day, it was actually worse after nightfall. At night, I would roll up in my poncho and try to rest. Sleep was impossible. It was dangerous in the countryside after nightfall. We were constantly told not to use any kind of light or even strike a match. It could make us a perfect target in the dark night. But there were still some GIs who would light up a cigarette and some of them were taken out by sniper fire. At night, we always had to assume that there might be Viet Cong watching us. We could be attacked at any time. There is nothing more terrifying than bullets screaming through the darkness when you can't see who is firing at you. I still know vets that even today can't sleep without a light on. I don't know how many rescue missions and patrols I survived without getting a scratch until finally my luck ran out.

On one mission as I went to help a soldier who was down, I felt a burning pain in my leg. But I could still walk and I was able to get him ready for the next chopper. When I sat down, a piece of shrapnel in my leg pushed through the skin and came out. I joined my patient on the next chopper. I came back to the ship as a patient instead of a corpsman, but fortunately my wounds weren't severe and I was able to get back to work in a week. Even if just for a week, being a patient gave me a different perspective. The recovery room was crowded and bunks were stacked three high. It was okay when I was really weak, but after I started to recover it was hard to lie down all day and not be able to get up and move.

For much of the time on patrol there was nothing to deal with but heat and humidity. A patrol could be out for a week and not encounter the enemy. But on the hospital ship, there was no escape.

The nurses and surgeons had to work twenty-four/seven. In my mind, they were the real heroes of the war. We would do our best to patch up the GIs and send them home, but sometimes the wounds were too severe and they didn't make it. At least the surgery we did for the orphans usually had a good outcome and sometimes we would play on the deck with the little toddlers. Some of the orphans were children of Vietnamese mothers and American soldiers. Their mixed race made them outcasts and that's why they were orphans. For us, those moments being with the children was a break from the war. We all felt good helping those kids.

There was one little guy that I became especially fond of. Nguyen Tugh's (I called him Tuff) cleft palate required a series of surgeries. When I would pick him up at the orphanage Tuff would play hide and seek with me. I would usually find him in the laundry chute though once the cook hid him in a giant soup pot. After I found him, he would jump into my arms and we would laugh and laugh. Those were the only times I laughed in Nam.

It was a sad day when we heard that the Viet Cong had overrun the orphanage. We didn't know how many children and nuns were murdered. I served almost two tours in Nam. I had seen some terrible things, but this time I cried.

The day after the massacre, as we walked through the orphanage, among the dead, we heard the moans and cries of wounded children. I ran to Tuff's hiding place and heard the faint sound of a little one crying. I found him in the laundry chute rolled up in the sheets. Tuff had always laughed with joy when I found him, but not that day. He gave me a smile and though weak from hunger and dehydration, he hugged me with every ounce of his strength. His head against my chest, we both cried as I carried him out of the ruins of the orphanage. As we moved to the chopper, I covered his head with my hat so that he wouldn't have to see the bodies of his friends. Along with the other survivors, we took Tuff back to the *Repose* and on to Danang where he was put in another orphanage. Tuff was only four years old and I often wonder what happened to him after the war.

This past winter, fifty years later, I was at the Marine Corps Museum in Quantico, Virginia with my two grandsons. I wanted them to know about the war. When I saw a display with a soldier scrambling out of a chopper as it touched down on the battlefield, it all came back and I couldn't talk.

I cried again and my grandsons hugged me.

SEVEN

> DEAR HELEN,
> *My loving wife,*
> *You know*
> *Living with me*
> *Isn't that easy*
> PTSD

ONCE I WAS STATESIDE, I was stationed at the Oakland Naval Hospital in the Inhalation Therapy Department. It had a big title, but it was boring and disgusting at the same time. All I did was wash and sterilize the machines after they were used. After a short stint I was able to transfer to the office of the Attorney Adjuntant.

I felt I was making a difference there. I worked with a civilian attorney and set up a program to help the Navy recoup some of the money that was spent on auto accidents involving military personnel. We recovered about one hundred thousand dollars from the insurance companies and got awards for the injuries of our patients.

When my tour of duty was over, the attorney that I worked with offered me a job to work with him in San Francisco. But I just wanted to go back home to Washington and put Vietnam behind me. And though I wouldn't admit it, in San Francisco, I was always looking over my shoulder. I was worried that I would run into the Lt.

Commander and his First Class Petty Officer goon. I had talked to the Naval attorney about the assault and he offered to prosecute. But I just wanted to get as far away as I could.

By then, my younger sister, Renette, who was just out of high school, was settled in Oakland. I took her to all the sites in the bay area and on some day hikes. Ever the protective older brother, I tried to pick the right places, but that didn't always work out. Down the coast at Half Moon Bay, a couple of guys, my roommate Pam, and Renette packed into my little sedan. At the trailhead we put some cheap wine, bread and cheese into our daypacks and headed down the trail toward the beach.

As we approached the shore, the view from the low cliff above the beach was beautiful. It was one of those perfect days, sunny, no wind and small waves and easy access to explore the tide pools. As we worked our way down the trail we could hear people laughing and yelling from the beach. When we came around the corner from an outcropping of rocks, I saw it was a nude beach. The sailors on the base were always trying to find the nude beach at Half Moon Bay. I had found it, but this was not the right time or place. I quickly spun Renette around and insisted we head back up the trail.

While I was in Oakland, I bought a 1951 Chevy pickup to do some landscaping for extra money. Unfortunately the engine gave up and the truck went to the junkyard. I loved that truck, but in short order I put some money down on my dream car, a four-year-old Mercedes Benz that I bought from one of my landscaping clients. As I left San Francisco and the military I drove up the coast singing Janice Joplin's, "Oh Lord, Won't You Buy Me a Mercedes Benz."

The car got me to Washington and the trip was great. But once I was home, I had to face another kind of music -- What do I do next? I didn't want to go back to nursing. In my mind nursing was tied into the war. So I got a job at the cedar shake mill. Ironically, packing bundles of shakes at the mill paid more than nursing did. Besides, working at the mill gave me more time to drink and raise hell. I was bitter and angry from all that I had seen and gone through in Vietnam. Hard work and drinking don't mix and I had several mishaps at work and eventually developed a cedar abscess in my lung from the cedar dust. At that point I decided to go back to school and clean up my act. If I continued as I was going, hell bent for nothing, I'd burn out pretty quickly.

But vows and actions sometimes differ.

On one of my footloose Fridays I left the Elks Club with many beers under my belt and I could barely stagger to my car. Still, being young, drunk and stupid, I headed home in the Mercedes. On the way home, I felt sick, hung my head out in the wind, and not surprisingly, the state patrol pulled me over. The officer came up to the window. He asked, "How are you tonight, sir?"

"Sick. I feel sick and I just want to get home."

He nodded and asked, "May I see your driver's license?"

I fumbled through my wallet, handed it to him. The officer looked at it carefully and asked, "Have you been drinking, Mr. Joseph?"

"Yes."

"How much have you had to drink tonight?"

I thought about saying, "Just a couple of beers" but I said, "I lost count. People kept buying me drinks and now I'm drunk as a skunk."

He had me get out of the Mercedes and led me back to his police car and opened the door to the back seat. After closing my door, he went around and got behind the steering wheel. Then he asked, "Where do you live, Mr. Joseph?'

"Behind the Catholic Church, up Monohan Hollow with Josie Monohan's family."

I expected to be booked for drunk driving, and then go to jail and pay a big fine. But the officer drove up to Josie's house and shut off the engine. Then he opened the back door and helped me as I stumbled up the porch and knocked on the door. Josie opened it and asked, "What's wrong, officer? Is John all right?"

"Mr. Joseph is too drunk to drive."

Josie looked confused. "Why here and not jail?"

He replied, "Years ago I promised myself that if I ever stopped someone for drunk driving and they admitted they were drunk instead of claiming they just had a couple of beers, I'd take them home and not to jail. It's been years and Mr. Joseph is the first."

The officer gave Josie my keys and I fumbled my way to bed. I guess sometimes, it's better to be lucky than smart. A couple of years after this, I was in school. I went salmon fishing to supplement my stipend from the GI Bill. My girlfriend, Helen, who would later become my wife, was with me as we towed the boat from the Willapa River back to Seattle. The overload of the trailer lights blew a fuse and it seemed that within minutes we were pulled over by the State Patrol.

As fate would have it, I quickly recognized Ed, the same officer who had pulled me over years before. I felt a little joke was in order so I said, "Who the hell do you think you are pulling me over? I ought to get out of this car and kick your ass!"

The officer smiled. "You're not big enough to kick anyone's ass," he said. Helen poked me and whispered, "Shut up or you'll end up in jail."

Slowly, I got out of the car. Ed looked me in the eye, laughed and gave me a big hug. Helen had been sure I was going to jail, but now she looked really surprised. We laughed a good little while as we drove out of town. Neither of us knew then that South Bend was going to be the place where we settled down. I did know, though, that old Ed was a gift. Not to mention Helen.

EIGHT

As I go out
Upon the sea
Grandmother Moon
Sleeps under
Her blanket
Of ocean green

IN 1973, being poor students, Helen and I decided to do our own wedding. I grew hanging baskets of beautiful fuchsias. Helen and her good friend, Linda, made all the layers for the wedding cake and stored them in freezers throughout the trailer park where we lived. Linda made Helen's wedding dress and my shirt. During the summer Helen picked up specials on roast beef and turkey. I fished during the summer and we had plenty of salmon for the reception.

But the day before the wedding, Helen and I got into a big argument. I don't even remember what it was about, but she and Linda took off. My mother had started cooking for the wedding, but now she was in tears. "What if she doesn't come back?"

I said, "We'll have a party. We already have all the food and drink that we need."

But Helen and Linda came back a few hours later and the

wedding was on. The next day as the guests began to show up we wondered where the minister was. Finally, an hour and a half late, the last one to arrive, the minister walked in stoned out of his mind. Bob was a minister for the street people of Tacoma. He was a friend and a great person. And he managed to do our wedding and sign all the papers, even stoned. After the reception we headed to Idaho Falls to visit some of Helen's family and then over to Moose, Wyoming to tell her parents that we had gotten married. We stayed at the trailer park and continued in school.

In 1976, I graduated from college, passed my RN license boards and took a job as a nurse practitioner for a local doctor in South Bend on the Washington coast in the same town where Ed had pulled me over for driving drunk.

Within a week, we sold the trailer for five thousand dollars. We used that for the down payment on a home in Bay Center, seventeen miles down the road from South Bend. The house cost twenty-five thousand dollars and we took on a mortgage of two hundred and fifty dollars a month. Built in the 1880's, it was a two-story saltbox that had only been owned by three families before us. Mr. Miller who built the house also built barges for the oyster beds along the bay. Mr. Bohaus, the second owner, added the tower and bay windows and also added some Victorian style trim. The third owner's wife dug the basement by hand before the brick foundation was put in to keep it from sinking into the clay.

It was cold and drafty, but we appreciated the romance of the old home and fell in love with it. We quickly became part of the community. Though I am Mohawk, I was adopted into the Chinook tribe so that I could help write grants for the community. Because there was only one other doctor in the area, I was really busy with new patients. If that wasn't enough to keep me busy, I became the owner of the *Uncle Marcia,* a thirty-two foot gillnetter for salmon fishing.

We named the boat after two people, Uncle Frank and Grandma Marcia. Uncle Frank was my adopted uncle and Grandma Marcia was my adopted grandmother. Despite the fact that neither of them was a blood relative, I couldn't have loved them more. Grandma Marcia, everyone in town called her Grandma, had been the nurse for the doctor who sold me his practice. She introduced me to all his patients, most of whom stayed because of her and showed Helen and me the intricacies of running the office. Helen took over management right from the start, and was incredibly good at it.

After he was discharged from the army in 1953, Uncle Frank moved in with his sister-in-law, Marcia. Uncle Frank ran some cattle and had a huge garden. When he hit social security age, he just kept on working the cattle. He was always working, only taking a break when someone needed a hand. He was there for everybody. It was a sad day when he died at the age of seventy-nine as a result of a heart attack. I helped Marcia sort things out. While cleaning out his truck, I found a stack of social security checks, all in their envelopes, all unopened. There were more in the glove box. We found the biggest pile in a desk drawer in the house. All told there was more than forty thousand dollars in checks that hadn't been cashed, not to mention several very large bank accounts with Grandma Marcia's name as survivor.

My good friend, Doc, a member of the Chinook tribe, had been fishing with me in an older boat that was always breaking down. Breakdowns make it hard to fish, but more than that, a breakdown at sea can be dangerous if the weather turns bad. Grandma Marcia bought a six- year old gillnet bow picker boat. It was a beautiful fiberglass boat designed and built by a boat builder in Bellingham. It cost thirty thousand dollars. She gave us a no interest loan to pay it off. For the rest of her life there would always be salmon in her refrigerator. Eventually, Grandma Marcia stopped working at the clinic when she was diagnosed with cancer. I would go over on my lunch break with medication for her. Though untrained, she was an accomplished artist and we would often paint together.

In those days during salmon season you could fish more than thirty days in a row. Since gillnetting is a type of salmon fishing that you could do with a one-man crew, Doc would fish during the day. I would fish all night and then go into the office at eight in the morning. I couldn't do that now, but I was young then. I could go the night without sleep, night after night. I used to motor out of the harbor and once I was out past the lights of town, I'd rev up the engine and head to the fishing grounds. On the front of a gillnet boat, there is a large reel with nets wrapped around it. When I threw the lever to free the reel, it would turn and drop the net overboard. Once the end of the net came free, I traveled slowly allowing the net to fall behind. Our net was two hundred and fifty fathoms, about fifteen hundred feet long, which is the length allowed by law. In ten minutes, the whole net would be in the bay. The bottom of the net had a weighted line attached and the top side had cork floats so the net hung in the saltwater like a fence.

While the net hung in the water for about an hour, I'd grab a mug of coffee from the galley and watch the stars revolving in the sky. Meanwhile fish swam into the fence and their gills got stuck in the netting. When an hour was up, I turned on the motor and started the reel rolling in reverse. The moment of truth was at hand. Would there be a lot of fish in the net or would I get skunked? Each set was different. Sometimes, if I got out and the weather was too rough, I didn't even bother to drop the net.

As the net rolled in, I picked out pieces of seaweed and debris. When I spotted a fish, I turned off the motor, plucked out the fish and tossed it down in the fish box layered with ice. After three or four sets, I headed toward the cannery just as the sun came up over the horizon. If the fishing was good, prices were low and if the fishing was bad, prices went up a bit more. I usually got a dollar a pound, but in the store it was six dollars a pound. Some of my patients couldn't pay much, if anything, so I used my fishing money to make ends meet.

We needed a place to store our nets in the off-season and one thing led to another. Helen and I bought a hundred-year-old empty church with a leaky roof that was across the street from our home. We replaced the roof and it became a good place to store nets. Each year, one hundred and twenty inches of rain falls on the island of Bay Center. The old church also became a gym where our kids would run and play while I mended the nets.

In time, we sold the old church to an artist; this was in 1992 and I believe it is still an art studio today. I stopped fishing when it got to be too much for me. I had several jobs at the time and it was a bit overwhelming. I was on the local school board, the local fire district commission, and I also served a term as county commissioner. I was a member of all the local organizations, and still working full time at our nurse practitioner's office.

Doc and I watched the fisheries getting depleted. We sold our fishing license back to the state so it wouldn't get used again. After that, Doc worked some oyster beds and then sold his share to his partner. Doc became a bear hunting guide over on the Quinalt Indian reservation. But he spent most of his time fighting for tribal recognition for the Chinook people. The government doesn't honor treaty rights with the Chinook, and like certain other tribes in the U.S., the recognition issue still goes on.

On occasion, I also testified in court as a medical consultant. I thought that most of the trials would be pretty dry affairs against an insurance company. But the first trial I testified at was a murder trial. In front of his three young children, a man in Grey's Harbor County killed his wife with a knife. After that, he drove to Seattle. He dropped the kids off at the police department, and confessed. I imagined that I was there to give some medical background about the wife's wounds. It was my first trial, a murder trial, and I was nervous when I took the stand. And then the judge asked, "Do you know what the McNaughton Rule is?" I knew that the McNaughton Rule defines the grounds for an insanity plea. But I was so nervous, that my mind flashed on McNaughton's Whiskey. I asked the judge: "Is that when you decide whether to pour one finger or two?"

He shook his head and went on with the trial but I could see he wasn't pleased with me. We should have stopped there because things went from bad to worse. The defense attorney looked like Willie Nelson. I had to restrain myself from humming *On The Road Again* and his questions bothered me. He had no case for his client and his strategy seemed to be an attack on my credentials. In a dismissive tone, he said, "You're just a nurse."

His shrug made me angry. I'd worked too hard to hear something like that, so I asked, "Who the fuck do you think you are? I am a licensed nurse practitioner in the state of Washington."

The judge pounded his gavel and gave me a lecture about court decorum. The judge was right, but I was still too "war angry" to put up with people like that. It was a good thing I hadn't planned on testifying in court very often, because they only called me a few more times. All three children were adopted by the same family and were able to stay together. But sadly, less than two years later, their adoptive mother died from cancer and those children had now lost two mothers. Their adoptive grandmother moved in and kept things going. The kids finished school and went on to college. We've stayed in touch with them over the years and the kids, now in their thirties, have families of their own.

When we moved into our office building, we assumed the lease the doctor had with the local hospital. We were proud that we were helping the residents of Pacific County, but after twenty years, the hospital wouldn't renew our lease. I think they wanted a "real doctor." As a result, they had nobody. They had an empty office. We were out on the street and who benefited from that? I sold the building to the hospital for what I had paid twenty years earlier.

We put our house up for sale and decided to move to the Olympic Peninsula. That was in 1995 and the house was appraised for two hundred and fifty thousand dollars. It stayed on the market seven years. We got tired of driving two hundred and twenty miles to cut the lawn and check on things. We loved the romance of that old home, but after we left, old wiring and old plumbing didn't hold the same charm. We spent twenty-two years restoring and remodeling that house, but we accepted an offer of eighty thousand dollars. The realtor said that an island, even one connected by bridge in Willapa Bay, was too remote to attract many buyers. Now, twenty years later, that same remoteness would be a big online selling point to a buyer in California, but not then.

Kittens playing with a feather
Puppies playing with a ball
Daughters in moms' old hats
Dresses dragging the floor
Children playing a role
Their innocence
More precious than gold

NINE

In 1995, after Helen and I sold the practice to the local hospital, we moved to a home between Port Angeles and Sequim up in the foothills of the Olympic Mountains. I took a job offer to work as a nurse practitioner at the Clallam Bay Prison. For a change, I could work for someone else and not have to manage a business. I felt successful and stable. I felt that I had finally left the Post Traumatic Syndrome Disorder (PTSD) from Vietnam behind me. The house was built in 1973. That might have been old to some people, but it was modern to us after moving from the Bay Center house that was over one hundred years old. It may not have had quite the character of the Bay Center house but there was more up-to-date plumbing and wiring. To me, that was a good trade-off. The house had a fireplace, a wood stove, and an electric furnace for heat. It would be cozy in the winter. It was up on a hill on ten secluded acres and there was room for a garden and a fruit orchard. Here was everything we needed. It was a perfect place for Helen and me and our two boys, Neaborn and Noel and our daughter, Sarah. It was peaceful. There would be no stressful events that would trigger my PTSD. I could leave Vietnam behind. I was at peace.

Two weeks after moving in, that inner peace left me when a pickup truck pulled into the driveway. Our house was off the beaten path. Our neighbors on each side of us had driven over to introduce themselves and a few friends had made a trip over to visit us. I was in the carport building some shelves for my tools as the truck came up the hill. When the truck door opened, I set my tape measure down and stepped out. The truck was so splattered with mud that I could barely make out the Green Crow Logging signs, but the man who climbed down was wearing clean jeans and boots. Even though he had a clipboard and a sheaf of papers in his hand, he was wearing the wide, heavy-duty red suspenders that loggers wear.

He put out his hand and said, "I'm Yankovich. I'm with Green Crow."

Now my boys liked their logo with a big green crow. "Yeah. I can see the sign. What can I do for you?"

Pointing down the hill, he said, "We need access to our property on the other side of the road."

"Going to do a clear cut?"

"You own a strip of land between the road and our property. We need you to sign over an easement to us so we can have access to our property."

"Tell you what. Green Crow owns a strip of land behind our place. I'm willing to trade that parcel with you. Green Crow would have access to their land and we would get protection for our property to the south of us from development and logging."

He shook his head. "That strip of land shouldn't even be in your parcel. It was surveyed, but the county put the road in the wrong place."

I shrugged. "Well, the mistake has been made. The road is where it is. Lucky for you that you caught me in a good mood and I'm willing to trade."

He handed me a pen. "Green Crow doesn't trade. Just sign this easement."

"Then we got no deal and Green Crow has no access."

"Lived here long?"

"Just two weeks."

"Yeah, well you'll learn. Timber runs this county."

I threw his pen on the ground and said, "Get off my property, before I call the sheriff."

As he climbed back in his truck, he laughed at me and said, "You just do that. Green Crow is real friendly with the sheriff."

I figured that was the end of it, but the next day on my way home from work, right across from my driveway, I saw skid marks leaving the asphalt. Someone had punched a road through our parcel of land on the other side of the road. I pulled my truck off to the side and went over to inspect. Some trees had been cut down to create a pathway. The ground was chewed up and the rain had turned it into mud. The mud almost sucked my shoes off, but I kept slogging on until I got to a clearing that wasn't there yesterday. Trees had been uprooted and pushed aside. In the center of the clearing there were two tractors and a log skidder.

Just as Yankovich had threatened, they were set to begin logging the next morning. I had seen enough and started back toward my truck. I hadn't gone very far before I hit a patch of mud that sucked off my shoe. That threw me off balance and I tumbled into the mud. I pushed myself up. I tugged at my shoe but couldn't free it from the mud and just left it behind. There was a light drizzle with a few snow flurries mixed in, but I was sweating beneath my jacket by the time I reached my truck. After I turned into the driveway, I gunned it up the hill. As I slammed the truck door, Helen stepped out of the house and shouted, "You're all covered in mud. You're missing a shoe. What the hell happened to you?"

I headed toward the house. "I'll explain later."

The boys were standing with her in the doorway, wide-eyed. She shook her head and said, "You're not coming in here covered in mud."

I nodded. "Right. Helen, while I collect some tools, do you think you can go back in the house and get some paper, some tape, one of the boy's markers and a sack of sugar?"

She raised her eyebrows. "This isn't about those tractors from Green Crow is it? The boys were down there watching and told me about it."

I nodded. She shouted, "I know what you're thinking, but you can't do this. Call the sheriff."

I shouted back, "Green Crow owns the sheriff!"

While we were arguing, the boys had gone into the house and

came out with paper, markers, tape, a sack of sugar that was still half full and even a pair of my boots. I thanked them, grabbed a couple of wrenches and a funnel, threw it all in the back of the truck and headed down the hill. A couple hours later, I came home tired, but it was a good tired. The boys came out and hosed me down with the garden hose. They laughed when I left my wet clothes in the garage and dried off with a towel. Helen wasn't laughing. "I hope you're pleased with yourself."

I grinned. "I sure am."

The next morning, the sun had barely come up but I was already out in the carport to organize my tools on the new shelves. On the end of the workbench, I had set a thermos and two mugs. I was expecting company. And sure enough, just when I poured myself a cup I heard a truck rumbling up the hill kicking up gravel. As it got nearer, I thought the truck might crash into our house, but Yankovich hit the brakes and leapt out of the truck. He slammed the door so hard, the mirror shook and I thought it might fall off. The veins in his neck were popping and he was red in the face. As he approached, I extended a mug toward him and asked, "Coffee?"

He had a piece of paper in his hand and shook his head violently. I took that as a, "No," and took the paper from his hand and said, "Good. I figured you would have noticed the funnel and the sugar that I left on the ground, but I taped this note to the cat just to be sure."

Yankovich snatched the note back and read it out loud. "There is sugar in the gas tanks."

He threw the paper on the ground, waved his finger at me and shouted, "Sugar in the tanks will destroy those engines."

I smiled. "Oh, you're right. Maybe you need to tow them back to the yard and drain the tanks."

Hearing the commotion, Helen stepped out of the house and when he started cursing, she called out, "I'm going to call the sheriff."

I nodded and she went back into the house. He screamed at me, "This is destruction of private property. I'm calling the sheriff!"

"No problem. My wife just called him. He can arrest you for trespassing, but I didn't put sugar in the tanks. I just left a note saying that I did."

Yankovich looked startled. "Why would you leave a note like that if it's not true?"

"So, you would come to your senses and save your equipment and just swap land parcels."

"You swear there is no sugar in the tanks?"

I took a sip of coffee and said, "There is no sugar in my coffee and maybe no sugar in your tanks. Now get those rigs off my property."

Yankovich frowned. I said, "Just have Green Crow's lawyer call and we can swap parcels."

"Green Crow doesn't give up land."

"Fine. They can buy the rights for fifty thousand dollars. Deal?"

Yankovich spit on the ground. "There's no deal, but don't think this is over by a long shot. Your boys..."

The hair on the back of my neck went up. "What about them?"

"Well, I noticed they like to come down and watch the big machinery. If they were to be playing on one of these big cats and got hurt, well that would be such a..."

"You son of a bitch!"

Time stopped. I didn't say a word, but I saw myself carving him up with my hunting knife. Yankovich seemed to sense how I was feeling. He took two steps back. I took three steps forward. I was right in his face and said, "If you ever hurt one of my boys, I will hunt you down and you will pay with your life."

He stepped back and said, "You're crazy. You'd go to jail for life."

"You're right. I am crazy; a crazy Vietnam Vet. Now get your rigs off my property and have Green Crow's lawyer call me."

Maybe a week later, to my surprise, a lawyer representing Green Crow called. I told him that they could have a one-time access for fifty thousand dollars. The offer would stay on the table but the price would go up five thousand dollars a day.

He hung up on me. We never heard from him again. We never heard from the sheriff either. But a few months later, Green Crow negotiated access with my neighbor across the street. I heard it cost them fifty thousand dollars.

TEN

Sun is the face of the Creator
That moves the tree tops
That directs the Wind
That moves the clouds

Day cools
Tree songs are quiet
Only crickets speak

Now Grandmother Moon
Spreads her blanket of night
And we place dream catchers
To capture nightmares and monsters

I HAD LEFT THE WAR TWENTY YEARS EARLIER, but the war hadn't left me. Though I didn't realize it at the time, my return to some of the Indian ways my grandparents had shown me was my pathway away from the war. Up the hill, behind our house there is a grove of alder and cedar trees. I made a little clearing there. I stripped the leaves and branches from some willow poles and bent them in a dome shape. I lashed the poles with deer hide strips where they crossed. But instead of the traditional buffalo robes, in a concession to the modern age, I covered the dome with thick felted blankets from the paper mill in Port Angeles.

I stepped back and viewed my handy work. Buffalo robes would have been better, but I felt that Pepé and Memé would have been proud. The next day, I dug a fire pit outside the lodge and collected large lava stones that I piled beside it. It was ready and I invited some friends from work to come over for a sweat lodge that weekend. Before they arrived, I built a fire. My grandson, Jonathan, and I put some large stones in the fire to heat up. By the time everyone arrived, the stones were glowing red. Using a pitchfork, Jonathan lifted some of the hot stones from the fire and put them in the center of the lodge. Four of us stripped off our clothes and sat in a circle around the glowing, red stones in the lodge.

I was the only Native American and none of the others understood the chants I sang as I put some sage on the hot stones and then ladled out water from a bucket to pour on the rocks. It was dark inside, but we could feel the steam rise and the lodge heat up. The heat didn't bother me, but the rule was that if it got too hot anyone was free to step out of the lodge. Sometimes people did. I felt at peace and I believe that even my friends who were not Native American felt at peace. I planned to have a sweat lodge once each season. Soon more and more people came and I held the sweats more often.

I don't know how word got out, but when Indians were traveling across the peninsula some of them would stop by for a sweat. Everyone was welcome. When other natives came we often put in another round of rocks to make it hotter. I thought I could handle the heat, but when a Comanche Indian visited I met my match. Jonathan loaded his pitchfork up with rocks and shoveled them into the center of the lodge, until there was a huge pile of glowing rocks. I kept pouring more water on them and the steam kept rising. As the sweat poured out of me, I somehow managed to stay, but some of the men opened the flap and crawled out. Those Comanche Indians do like it hot!

I am from the Mohawk tribe, one of countless tribes that populated North America for thousands of years. Of the many tribes that once existed, some are lost forever. The remaining tribes are smaller in number. Where our ancestors might once have been members of warring tribes, all of us here today are survivors. Tribes are distinct but we respect our differences and learn from each other. The Mohawks are from the Northeast, but today I live in the Pacific Northwest. Pepé wanted to learn from Frank Fools Crow and so Pepé and I made countless trips to see him in South Dakota. As I strive to regain my tribal heritage, I also feel kinship with and respect for all the other tribes that are still struggling to survive.

The sweat lodge helped me reconnect to the world of my ancestors, but the ceremony with the deepest spiritual meaning to the Native American Plains People is the Sun Dance ceremony. Though once outlawed, the ceremony continued in secret, before the legal ban against it was finally dropped in the 1970's. Before the Sun Dance ceremony itself, the first time dancers go through an ordeal of purification sweat lodge and fasting that lasts four days. I did that before my first ceremony, but the Sun Dance ceremony goes in groups of four, one for East, West, North and South. By now I have done eight ceremonies.

The ceremonies I have gone to eight times were with the Shoshone Bannock and Lakota People in Montana and Idaho. It is a long sixteen hour drive from my home on the Olympic Peninsula, but I know I am approaching my destination when I get to Hell's Half Acre. Despite the name, it's one hundred and fifty square miles. It is an ancient lava lake with many lava tubes and is made up of multiple lava flows. It's hard to imagine that anything can live in those lava flows, but there are walking trails and even on a short hike, I have seen countless plants that have taken root including sage, wheat grass, ferns, Indian paintbrush and prickly pear cactus. Wildlife is also abundant. On the same hike, it would not be surprising to see bobcat, coyote, golden eagles, mule deer, red foxes and plenty of sage grouse.

I love to stop and walk through the lava beds, but on the last trip, my eighth ceremony, it was still dark. Wanting to be at the Sun Dance ceremony by sunrise, I kept driving and arrived at the encampment just as the sun was coming up over the horizon. There was a mix of tepees and nylon tents and whiffs of smoke drifting up from some of the campsites. I worked my way to the Sun Dance circle and though I hadn't called ahead, Violet was already at the circle waiting for me. In her eighties, she has large brown dancing eyes and wears a broad smile. Violet is a women's spiritual leader and she has been my sponsor at each Sun Dance.

The intercessor, the guide, the sacred person who intercedes on behalf of the people, was sitting on an elk skin robe with his smudging shell in one hand and eagle feather in the other. Facing the sun, he was singing a greeting to the Creator. The smell of sweet grass, cedar, and Indian tobacco from the smudging shell permeated the air. I changed from my t-shirt and walking shorts into a deer hide dance skirt. Cliff, whose Indian name was Jumping Leg, handed me a smudging shell and a fan. Standing next to the intercessor, I sang my greeting to the Creator. Maybe a dozen others who were going to dance had joined us. We all sat soaking up the warmth of the sun for about an hour as we sang our welcome songs and prepared ourselves for the ordeal of Sun Dance.

Cliff stood up and walked to the arbor that had been built to provide shade for elders who were there to support the men who would dance that day. I was the oldest dancer of the group. The others were young men in their early twenties who were dancing for the first time. As first time dancers, they had already been through the four-day ordeal of purification sweat lodge and fasting. Cliff signaled for us to come to the arbor to be pierced and attached to the tree with the lines that were secured to the top.

I was second in line for the piercing. To distract from the pain, I blew on my eagle bone whistle as Cliff took his knife and made parallel cuts on the right side of my chest. He then forced a piece of buffalo bone through the slits in my flesh. He did the same thing on the left side of my chest. Violet tied the lines from the tree to the pieces of bone and I was ready for the dance. I continued to blow on my eagle bone while I danced back and forth to the tree. Each time I danced backward as far I could in order for the bones to tear through my flesh and free me. The drumming and singing rolled over the circle and filled our bodies with the heartbeat of mother earth. But after three times to the tree and back, I needed a rest. Violet had already made me a resting place in the arbor with a bed of fresh picked sagebrush tips. There was a fruit jar full of water for me next to a post that I leaned back on.

It would have been easy to fall into a deep sleep, but after a short rest, I returned to the dance. It took me three hours to tear loose from the pole. Violet was right there with cold washrags to wash the dust and dirt off my wounds. By then it was ninety-five degrees and she also brought me a bowl of cold watermelon. I had fasted for forty-eight hours and the watermelon was good. I was tired, but I was at peace and I could easily have stayed at the celebration that went on after all the dancers had torn loose, but Violet had other plans. She said, "I am concerned for George. We need to check on him."

George was once a young man, but that was some twenty-five hundred years ago. I met George through a doctor who had a passion for archeology. The good doctor had dug up the remains of the man that I had nicknamed George. The doctor stored George's remains in a shoebox in his basement. He asked me to take the remains back to the reservation for a proper burial. I told Violet about George at an earlier Sun Dance and I found a burial site at what I thought had been an ancient ceremonial site. There were numerous petroglyphs with shaman symbols. I buried George's remains in the traditional way. I wrapped him in red felt, placed him in a small cave and covered the entrance with rocks and brush.

Violet wanted to see the burial site I had made for George. Violet asks so little of me, so I changed back into my shorts and t-shirt and we headed north up past Mud Lake to the valley between the Bitter Root Mountains. It was daylight, but as we drove though Indian Valley we could see the moon resting on top of the mountains. We rode in silence for seventy-five miles, before we turned onto a dirt road and drove for another ten miles into the desert. It was warm when we started walking, but we climbed three hundred feet to the petroglyphs. Violet studied the cliff paintings for a long time. Concerned that the heat and the climb might be too much for her, I said, "We don't have to continue."

She shook her head. "Yes, we do. We can't leave that boy alone."

Violet slowly made her way up the hill and in about forty-five minutes we reached the top. I pointed toward the cliff wall and said,

"George is over there."

I cleared away the brush and rocks that I had placed there on my last visit. Violet began to sing a mourning song as she picked up each bone and carefully put them in a deerskin pouch. The red felt that I had left with the bones was gone. Violet said, "Someone has found this site."

I thought it could have been one of those pesky desert rats, but she might have been right. There are many little caves in the basalt rocks. I prepared another small cave while Violet sang a mourning song and smudged the remains. As she placed them into the new burial site, Violet turned toward me and asked, "Do you hear someone singing?"

I nodded. It was a young man's voice singing in a language that I had never heard. I looked up and down along the ledge. There was no one in sight. I did not even see any dust kicked up. Violet finished smudging the remains and we put the rocks in front of the entrance to the cave. The singing continued as we made our way down the hill and back to the car. When we got back in the pickup, we sat with the windows down and listened to the singing. Suddenly, it stopped. Only then did I start the pickup. I felt sad as we drove out of the desert, but Violet said, "It was good the ancestors came to sing for him."

ELEVEN

WHILE FAMILY, FRIENDS AND MY INDIAN HERITAGE HELPED ME SURVIVE my return from Nam, other vets had nothing and they suffered greatly. I was still happy that we had moved to the Olympic Peninsula, but even with a new job and a new house, I was unable to leave the war behind. So I volunteered to do medical exams for vets at the counseling office in Port Angeles. But not all the vets that needed our help were coming in. They didn't trust anyone including doctors. Since I was a vet, the counselor thought they might trust me and asked if I would hike into a camp where some of the Vietnam veterans were supposed to be living. There was an urban legend that maybe up to one hundred Vietnam vets were scattered in illegal camps up in the mountains inside Olympic National Park. Maybe it was really true.

Bruce, the counselor at the center, told me some of the guys actually got off the plane and moved directly into the camps without going home or seeing their families. Some of them had wives and kids, but couldn't cope with life after Vietnam. They just checked out of society and moved into the camps. Bruce introduced me to George who was making a daily run to check points where the men in the camps would leave messages in a coffee can in culverts or stumps along the road.

Most of the time, the message was just a list of things they needed like coffee, sugar, flour and soap. Sometimes, it might be a request for aspirin, ibuprofen, cough syrup, vitamins and other over the counter medications and maybe a request for a candy bar. Occasionally, a note would state that one of the vets was sick or injured and needed some help. Once George went into one of the camps to bring out a guy who had suffered a heart attack. Unfortunately, the vet, who went by the name of Mack, died on the journey out of the mountains.

George told me, "It was a ten mile hike to the camp, mostly downhill, but uphill going back out. Mack refused to let us make a litter and drag him out. Mack was insistent there be no helicopter or rescue party. He didn't want to expose the campsite to the park rangers."

George sighed. "It was obvious Mack was having a lot of chest pain and couldn't breathe. Every step was labored. Finally he collapsed and took his last breath. There was nothing I could do out there in the woods, but I still blame myself."

After George left, Bruce asked, "There is man named Jack in one of the camps who is really sick. Will you go?"

I had no gear with me, but we made a trip to the Goodwill for some clothing more suitable for roughing it in the woods. Bruce gave me a sleeping bag and a backpack to use. My medical bag was always with me and the old Navy and Marine Corpsman within me, as much as I had tried to put it out of mind, came alive. George took me to the trailhead. He had arranged for Aaron, who lived at the camp, to guide me in.

The hike to the camp was about eleven miles. It wasn't bad at first, but the last three to five miles was a killer. The trail was steep with lots of switchbacks and we must have climbed another three thousand feet. My pack was small and only weighed twenty pounds, but Aaron's was huge and I asked, "Why do you carry such a big pack?"

He said, "The rangers turn a blind eye to our camps, but if they change their tune or if someone stumbled across the camp while I was gone, I would lose everything. So, whenever I leave camp, I pack it all up. Everything I own is in this pack."

We arrived at the camp as the sun was going down. It was a nice September day, in the mid-seventies, but in the mountains, the temperatures would drop into the thirties at night. Not good for a sick man. We went to Jack's lean-to. He was shivering in his sleeping bag and appeared to be in a lot of pain. I set my bag down and checked my supplies. I had plenty of bandages, aspirin and ibuprofen. I had some sterile instruments to suture a wound and a couple of syringes and some Xylocaine if I needed to do a local anesthetic. I also had some amoxicillin and erythromycin to treat a low-grade infection.

I introduced myself and said, "I understand you have been injured with an axe. Show me your wound."

Jack pulled his right leg out from his sleeping bag. He had on two pairs of sweat pants and long underwear. Even so, the infected leg smelled of rotting meat. It was over-powering and it was all I could do not to gag. The lower leg of the sweat pants was soaked in pus and blood. I cut away the clothing and exposed the wound. The wound was about six inches long and the axe had hit a bone in his lower leg. I caused a lot of pain just cutting away the clothing.

I injected the wound with Xylocaine though I didn't know if it would work since so much infection had set in. It had to hurt but he just kept shivering. Jack had a high fever. He was in septic shock and needed immediate medical attention. I numbed up the area around the wound and covered up his leg with a clean towel. Jack seemed to relax and I crawled out of the tent. I looked around the campsite. There was an elaborate water system with water being delivered to camp via a cedar plank flue from a nearby creek. A communal fire ring was in the center of the camp with tents set around the fire pit.

The men had dug a latrine about one hundred yards away. It was a three-walled shelter with a split cedar roof. Without a door, there was a beautiful view of the mountains. There was even some toilet paper next to the toilet seat that had been carried in. But more impressive was the effort expended to haul in a fifty-pound sack of lye to sprinkle in the hole periodically. Aaron stepped up and said, "This is Matt."

As I shook Matt's hand, Aaron said, "This is the doc who has come to see Jack."

Matt just nodded. I asked him, "Would you mind heating up some water for me so I can clean up Jack's leg?"

He didn't answer, but picked up a bucket, got some water from the flue and set it over the fire. When the water was warm I added some dish soap. I cleaned the wound with warm, soapy water and Jack seemed to relax a little more. With the wound clean, I could see that there was a lateral fracture to the fibula, the smaller of the two bones in the lower leg. The tissue around the bone was infected and it was likely the infection had spread to the bone itself. I said, "Jack, we need to call in a rescue crew and get you to the hospital. There is a good chance that you might lose the leg otherwise."

Matt said, "We can drag him out on a litter, but it's up to Jack."

I said, "I don't think the antibiotics will clear up the infection. You need some high-powered shit that I don't have. How about it, Jack? Will you let the guys take you out and get you to the hospital?"

Jack finally turned back toward me. "No. I ain't going to the hospital. If I'm going to die, I want to do that right here. Besides, I don't need the hospital. I'll be okay with what you're doing."

I wasn't so sure, but there was no way to convince him. I applied the warm soapy compresses once an hour and gave him the antibiotics. In the morning, I asked him, "Jack, why did you move out here to the camp instead of staying in town?"

He said, "When I got back from Nam I got a job at the mill, but I didn't fit in. At work I would hear men yelling and think I was under fire. Everything had changed. Nothing was right. I would wake up at night with nightmares. I could only sleep two hours at a time. My wife would yell, 'Just get over it!'

"She had no idea what was going on in my head. Hell, half the time I didn't know what was going on in my head. Then when one of my buddies and I were out drinking, he took a corner too fast and we hit a tree. He went through the windshield and died. We went to high school together, but I just couldn't face his parents. I came up to visit Matt and Aaron just to get away for bit, but I couldn't go back. My granddad used to say when he was fed up with the government, just fed up with life, he would say, 'The dirt in my shoes don't belong to me no more.'

"The dirt don't belong to me no more. My heart is willing to go back, but my soul is too weary. I need to sleep on the ground."

But at least Jack was eating and drinking and the swelling in his leg and foot was going down. After seventy-two hours his wound was looking better and my family needed me at home. As I was packing my medical bag, Jack said, "We don't get many visitors and they hardly ever return. I hope you won't forget us."

Being at the camp with those other vets and listening to Jack brought back so many ugly memories of Vietnam. While it was painful to be at the camp with those vets who could never fit in and had dropped out of society, I knew where I was needed and where I wanted to stay. The corpsman in me pushed down and out to civilization to restock my medical bag for the next trip in.

The story of Noah and the Ark
Moses and the Jews
Jesus, Mary and Joseph
All tales twice told

I think of softsoap politicians
And their twice told tales
Of hope and help to widows,
Veteran's children

All of whom listen with hope
And it is time for mothers to control
The government that doesn't listen
That doesn't have ears

To hear its own twice told tales
I believe it is time to keep promises
To keep peace
To heal the wounds
That refuse to heal

It is Memorial Day, I stand in the rain
Rain drops from my eyes
Mysteries of the seas
Fallen comrades

We carry the mysteries
Of the brotherhood
Between soldiers and sailors
Because only they understand

What it means to lose everything
To live the story, to see the story
Not once but twice
Twice told tales

TWELVE

ONCE A WEEK, FOR THE PAST THREE DECADES, I would stop at a designated spot on the highway and check the coffee can under the culvert to see if there was a message for me. If there was a message that week, and there usually was, I packed up my medical bag and hiked in to see the guys. As much as a dose of antibiotics and vitamins, the men needed human warmth. When my twin boys got older, I would sometimes bring them with me. The men missed children in their lives and they couldn't have been kinder to my boys.

Just like me, the men in the camps had been naïve when they were shipped to Vietnam. Scared for our lives, we fought in a war that was a mistake from day one. On our return home, it hurt when people hurled insults at us as we stepped off the plane. And worse than that, they ignored us as we tried to settle back into our old lives. If people had thanked us, maybe some of those men would have gone back home instead of fleeing to the woods.

I was lucky. I had Pepé and Memé to hear my stories and share my pain and help me step back into life. Otherwise, who knows? I might have joined them in the mountains. Anyway, while I still check, it's been at least five years since there has been a message in the coffee can for me. We have all grown older, but they lived a harder life than me. I suppose some died in the mountains and others came down to nursing homes to finish out their lives. But in case there is even one man still in the mountains, I keep checking.

Last year Richard, the co-author of this book, and I hiked into where one of the camps had been. When I was in Vietnam he was suspended from college for blocking military recruiters from entering the administration office. We were so young. We would not have been friends back then, but now our shared effort has brought us together. He is a good friend and the two of us went to find some of the old vets, give them a voice and tell their stories. It seems we were too late. The camp was empty. Nature had taken over and healed the scars that were left in the earth.

Except for a hollow dug in the ground for a long ago campfire, there was no evidence that men had ever lived there while trying to sort out the war and make sense of their lives. I know their struggle because I have yet to make sense of the war. The best I can do to honor those men is live my life the best I can. Not forget. Not ever forget. Not ever.

My grandfather, Pepé, has passed away, but as we stood at the edge of the lake where men, cast away by society, lived out their lives, I heard Pepé's voice. I could smell the cigar smoke from his shirt as he said, "Everything is a gift from the Creator. Life itself is the greatest gift of all."

EPILOGUE

I HAD HOPES that if I got my story into print, it would help people. Even if it helped just one person, I would be happy. But the story developed in fits and starts. In the beginning, the plan was for Richard to take my shoe box full of papers; a jumble of journal entries, essays and poems going back thirty years and totaling four hundred plus pages and organize them into a book. It was all there. How hard could it be? It wouldn't take long... But somehow, the weeks became months and the months became years. As John Lennon said, "Life happens while you're making plans."

Part of it was because of me. Part of it was because of Richard. He could have just punched the "send" button and I would instantly have a copy of his latest pages to review. We live in the digital age, but that's not me. This man who was going to write the story of my life, I had to know who he was. Instead of punching "send," I would say, "Just print up your pages and drive over to my place."

Richard lives about forty miles down the road. The road to my house climbs up towards the Olympic Mountains and ends at the boundary of the Olympic National Park. It's a nice drive although occasionally in the winter there is snow at my property because of the elevation. But in the fall, during mushroom season when he brought out a few pages, we would head out and collect mushrooms. The first time out, as we filled a basket, Richard asked, "Are you sure these are the safe kind of mushrooms?"

I know what I am doing in the woods, but I just shrugged and said, "Well, this isn't Safeway, but we'll know for sure within a couple of hours."

Of course, when we got back to my house, I would make a mushroom stew. And the five pages that I could have read in ten minutes became an all day visit after collecting, chopping mushrooms and finally breaking bread over a bowl of stew. Sometimes, I camped at the state park that is only a mile away from Richard's house. And then I would go over to his home to visit and to collect some pages. Or he might bring a bundle of firewood to my campsite and we would sit around the fire. On one of those visits, I helped him launch his boat. It's a two-person rowing boat, a fourteen-foot Whitehall. It just cuts through the water, but is pretty tippy. Even with my Parkinson's disease in the early stages, I was afraid I was going to fall out when I climbed out of the boat. Richard, who is just a few years younger than me, is healthy and fit. He had recently retired from teaching PE and led aerobics everyday, but he kept up a morning workout routine that included twenty push-ups. He had no trouble at all. I'm not sure if he noticed or if he was just too kind to say anything.

Despite our slow ways, we finished the manuscript about a year ago. Before we could try to find a publisher, Richard went to the desert, but instead of taking desert hikes his trip turned into the vacation from hell. He became extremely sick and when his wife, Jody, got him home and to the ER, he was diagnosed with bacterial meningitis. He said, "I had just wanted to take a nap, but Jody insisted on taking me to the ER."

From my years in medicine, I know that disease. About twenty percent don't survive it. Of the survivors, a third have trouble walking again and another third have difficulty speaking. For others, memory can be a problem. The recovery is similar to what stroke victims face. He survived, but after eight days in the hospital, he left twenty pounds lighter. I said, "Jody was right. You never would have woken up. Don't you just hate it when your wife is right and you are wrong?"

Richard laughed. "But as you said, she saved my life."

He was so thin and weak that I could have pushed him over with one hand. "Now I push my walker across the living room and then I have to take a nap."

"Naps are good."

"Not a four hour nap! Why did this happen?"

"My grandfather Pepé would say, 'It's all a gift.'"

He shook his head and said, "I can't see it that way."

The next time I saw him, he had traded in his walker for some walking sticks. I took that as a good sign and said, "You're going the right direction. It must have felt good to turn in the walker."

"It did, but…"

He paused. I waited, but finally asked, "But what?"

"Sorry. Sometimes, it's hard to get the words out. Will that change?"

"There are no certainties."

"You know, when Jody took me to the ER, they thought they were missing my hospital records. I don't take any medications and it was more than fifty years since I was in the hospital to have my appendix removed."

"There's the world of the healthy and the world of the sick. What have you seen on your visit to my world?"

We were sitting in a restaurant and my service dog, Snickers, was resting under the table with his head on my feet. Richard put his coffee cup on the table and said, "A couple of weeks ago I was pushing my walker across the bank parking lot. It wasn't easy to navigate the cracks in the asphalt. I have been going there for thirty years, but I had never noticed. Some people will always need to use a walker and have to struggle with that everyday of their lives. I'm lucky."

"You see things you didn't see before. That is your gift."

I see life as a gift. I'm in my seventies. I wish I had seen it earlier, but maybe it's the right time in my life to look back and try to make sense of things. Richard and I have been collaborating on this book for over four years. That shared effort led to a friendship. We don't talk just about the book anymore. We talk about lots of things. I wondered if Richard had thoughts like that too. So I asked him, "How do you see your life now?"

"I am starting to see it as a circle. At first, rehab was really difficult. I just didn't have enough strength to do the exercises. But the pool has a therapy swim. I used to swim laps five or six times a week but I had lost so much weight and my circulation was so poor that now I had to wear a wetsuit to stay warm. On my first day there, I tentatively walked into the pool and held onto the wall. Molly, the lifeguard, smiled at me in encouragement. I recalled that when I taught swimming years earlier, and she was six years old, I rescued her when she strayed into the deep end. I hoped she wouldn't have to do the same for me."

"Did rehab help?"

"It did, but it was the people at the pool who made the difference. They were all supportive. Tristan, one of the lifeguards, had been in my high school PE class. I didn't know it then, but he had meningitis when he was nine years old. He couldn't walk for three months, but he persevered. It was as if our experiences made us members of a small club."

"A club that neither of you would choose to join."

"Right, but we had that shared experience and he encouraged me. After a few months I thought I was ready to try one of his water aerobic classes. It was more difficult than it used to be for me, but I made it through the class. At the end, Tristan smiled and said, 'We've come full circle. You used to lead our aerobics class in PE. Now I am the teacher and you are the student.'"

"I guess we have to try to find our place in the world as we get older."

Richard nodded, "I remember watching my granddaughter, Sophie, when she was only a year old, pulling a pillow off our kitchen bench, dragging it down the hallway and into the bedroom and then pushing it onto the bed with the other pillows. It struck me that she was trying to create a sense of order in her world. Our world is much bigger now, but I guess we still need to see where we fit in."

"I see life as a gift. You see it as a circle. That's maybe not so different. I guess, just like your granddaughter, we both have a need to create some sense of order out of the chaos in our world. I bet we're not alone there."

~

Eleven years ago when I retired, I looked forward to peace and quiet. No early morning commute. No work stress. I would have time to relax and do nothing. That was the plan. The reality is that now I work full time and don't get paid. Instead of one paid job, I have three volunteer jobs. I work at the office of the DAV, Disabled American Vets. I help guide vets through the process of getting help, financial and medical from the Veterans Administration. They fought for our country. Many of those vets have lived with physical and emotional pain for decades. And now they have to fight the VA to honor the promises of care that were made to them. I love to step in and fight for them. We used to call it war anger. When I came back from Nam, I would fly off the handle at the slightest thing that didn't go right. Over the years I've learned to channel that energy into "the right fight". And fighting for our vets is the right fight. I also teach three exercise classes at the pool. And I work at the Free Clinic that serves the poor and homeless.

Along with that, Helen and I have raised two grandchildren, Jonathan and Lindsey. They moved out after high school and are on the way to establishing their own lives. We are really proud of them. Helen and I are getting older. I've got health problems and people wonder why I do so much. Well, I don't want to be a burden to anyone. I tell myself that maybe if I keep moving, keep working, I can hold off age and health issues for a while. And yes, I know that won't last forever. In Washington, when your health is bad enough it is legal to get help for assisted suicide. It is called the Death with Dignity Law. I know some people that have gone that route. For most people it's about control. Seventy-five percent of the people who get that packet of pills don't use them. But they take comfort in knowing that they will have control of their last days. And I'm glad we have that choice.

Pepé taught me that there will be moments of joy and pain, but everything, everything, is a gift. As is true for many Native Americans, my ancestors converted to Catholicism. Many generations ago, those early conversions came about when the choice was to accept the white man's religion or face death. Even when the choice was not always so stark, as native cultures lost their sacred lands and were decimated by diseases brought over from Europe, our communities faced great pressures. In those desperate times, indigenous people converted to the new religion that offered hope in another life. I think as in most formal religions, as they grow and expand, money and power corrupts. Though I grew up with it, Catholicism does not give me comfort.

I see so many vets returning from war and questioning how God could let such terrible things happen. Formal religion does not seem to give them any comfort either. At the same time, they so want to find something bigger than themselves. Many vets come to our ceremonies. I think a sweat lodge, with the heat, and the dehydration and the camaraderie is more hands on and might be more tangible for them than the feeling they would get by giving ten percent to the church each week. Maybe some of them can find peace by being close to nature. A vet who no longer goes to church told me, "When I look at a beautiful sunset, I can feel the power of God."

Some Native Americans resent white people coming to our ceremonies, but most are welcome if they come to learn from us. My two adopted twin boys are red-haired and fair-skinned, but they were always welcome at the ceremonies. My grandfather Pepé and even Frank Fools Crow, a great Lakota spiritual leader, would say, "Everyone is welcome to come and embrace the spiritual ways of the past peoples." From what I have seen, the reward of heaven and the threat of damnation in hell does not address what most frontline, battle veterans have been through. Communing with nature in a spiritual way allows for some peaceful moments in their shattered souls.

I have had maybe thirty or forty mothers who are not Native American ask me to make a medicine bag for their sons to protect them as they headed off to war in Iraq or Afghanistan. I make the medicine bags from a tanned buffalo skin or deerskin. On each bag, I sew beads in the design of a goat, a shaman, or deer tracks. Their sons might put in an earring from their wife or a lock of hair from their baby, something of meaning to them. The medicine bags were against military regulations so they would wear them under their uniform. In 2006, the military changed regulations to allow them on religious grounds. I can't prove that they offered protection, but all of the men who wore the medicine bags came home alive.

Many people are looking for something that organized religion can't seem to give them. Yet, I see some people, as they approach death, go back to the church. One never knows, but when my time comes I don't think I will do that. Sometimes, I think that with my medical background, I know too much. I know the progression of Parkinson's disease and the toll it will take on me and on my family. It's hard, but I just have to trust in the Creator.

In this country, we have eighteen vets a day that take their own lives. There are twenty active service members that take their lives each day. It is a waste and so sad. I want to stick around and fight for them as long as I can. I try to be positive. That is a choice I can make and I think that will help me heal. I take comfort in the wisdom of a firefighter I met through my work at the Free Clinic. She was taking care of her eighty-year-old mother and she told me, "We are here to help walk each other home."

TRADE LANGUAGE

I DON'T PRETEND TO BE A LINGUIST, but I see a lot of similarities in the East Coast Trade Language and the West Coast Chinook Jargon. Both the East and the West coast Jargons contain a lot of European words, Asian words, and even Russian words mixed with Native American Sign Language and local tribe words. Native Americans found the Dutch language difficult to pronounce. So, it was the French fur traders who had the most influence on the Trade Language. In fact, all European white men were called French. There are a lot of European words in the English we speak that are not from the Queen's English. For that matter, as time has gone by, Asian and Middle Eastern words have also added to the vocabulary of Americanized English. In a way, the American English that we know has become its own Trade Language or Jargon.

It is sad to me that we are losing the Native American Trade Languages just as we have lost many of the traditional Native American tribal languages. I am a good example of that. I failed to teach my children the Trade Language, as I knew it, and have forgotten most of it over the sixty-two years I have been away from my grandparents. I thought I would teach my children while they were infants, but it did not work out. I was so busy working to support the family I did not take the time to teach them.

Tony Johnson, a renowned Pacific Coastal artist and a member of the Chinook Tribe, has revived the Chinook Jargon and has taught his children as they have grown up to speak the Jargon fluently. He holds classes at the Chinook Tribal Center to teach the Jargon to other members of the tribe and he has been very successful in bringing the Jargon back to life. It is used frequently at Tribal Ceremony and events. There is a Trade Language book on the Chinook Jargon, *Chinook: A History and Dictionary* by Edward Harper Thomas, Binfords and Mort Publishers, Portland Oregon.

Here is a glossary of some of the Trade words that I remember.

To work, the act of doing anything	Mamook
To run fast, to bring, to fetch	Mamook chako
Aunt	Tata
Hello	Sakan
Down	Couche
Frying pan or stove	Lapoel
To fry, to cook	Mamook lapoel
Straight, direct, true	Delate
To speak the truth, direct, true	Dealte wawa
Much, plenty, abundance	Hiyu
Small number	Teans hivu
Run, play, walk travel	Cooley
Run fast	Hyah cooley
To stop, to halt	Kopet cooley
White man	Frenchman
Any white man other than French	Dutchman
French origin	Lapell
Shovel	Pelle
Shovel or spade	Lapell
Ghost, spirit, goblin	Tahmahnowis
Dog	Kamooks
Door	Lapote
Tree	Tabacco
Can	Kahn
Turtle	Keya
Friend	Six

THANKS

I WANT TO THANK Gerry and Lorry Hausman of Irie Books who have been supportive of me in this endeavor from the very beginning. Steve Gillard, Virgil Rondeau and Derrell and Lynne Sharp all read the story and offered helpful suggestions. In addition, Derrell and Lynne contributed valuable information about the Vietnam War and salmon fishing. John's wife, Helen, read the manuscript and was most helpful with details and recounting incidents that took place. I am grateful for the efforts of my wife, Jody, who has read the story at every stage and offered support and encouragement to help me make this story the best it could be. Jacque Peters and Robert Donaldson from Port Townsend Computers were always there when I needed tech support. Jack Blake from Imagination to Imagery Photography was very helpful with some photos that we used for publicity. He also shared ideas for the cover.

There have been many others who have been supportive and helped bring this book to print. I also want to thank Carl Adams, Dennis Lemaster, Jim and Debbie Hampton, James Sanderson, Rich Chaney and Kathy Barnett Chaney, Michael Sullivan, Rob Brooke and Mark Anderson. John Joseph entrusted me with his life's story. Working with John has been a collaborative effort. We talked, we argued and we talked some more. In the end, we finished a book and began a friendship. You can't ask for more than that.

— R G

ABOUT THE AUTHORS

JOHN JOSEPH, a Vietnam veteran, was born to a Native American father and English/Irish mother. He has been married for forty years to Helen, the love of his life. Together they have raised five children.

John graduated from Seattle Pacific University and worked as a family nurse practitioner. His volunteer work includes teaching classes at the city swimming pool, helping veterans and widows/widowers through Disabled American Veterans, and helping the homeless and uninsured at a free medical clinic.

In his spare time, he enjoys painting landscapes and portraits and working in his pottery studio.

RICHARD GLAUBMAN is the author of *Life is So Good* and *More Than a Book; a Story of Friendship*. He was a teacher for three decades during which he taught students at every grade level from pre-school to community college. He lives with his wife, Jody, on the Olympic Peninsula in Washington State.

Also by Richard Glaubman:

LIFE IS SO GOOD
In this remarkable book, George Dawson, a slave's grandson who learned to read at 98 and lived to the age of 103, reflects on his life and shares valuable lessons in living, as well as a fresh, firsthand view of America during the entire sweep of the twentieth century.

MORE THAN A BOOK: A STORY OF FRIENDSHIP
Narrated by Richard Glaubman, this book recounts what happened to both men after Dawson's life story was published. During their time together on a national book tour, despite differences in age, race and education, the friendship begun in a humble kitchen in South Dallas grew even stronger.